Astral Projection

Your Personal Guide to the Astral World

(Proven Techniques and Methods for Learning to Travel Astral Plain)

George Costilla

Published By **Region Loviusher**

George Costilla

Astral Projection: Your Personal Guide to the Astral World (Proven Techniques and Methods for Learning to Travel Astral Plain)

ISBN 978-1-998927-37-1

Legal & Disclaimer

Table Of Contents

Chapter 1: Starting Out

After a person falls asleep, the astral body projects into the physical dimension. It can move around freely, but it is limited by the energy field of the expanded physique. This field is called cord activity range. This is the phase when a person tries to project into the Astral Dimension in his consciousness. This phase is often overlooked by beginners. Etheric Matter All living beings contribute to the production of matter that is responsible for life force. This material is called Etheric. It can be physical or astral. Recent scientific studies have confirmed the existence of this matter, as it carries weight. A person who dies loses a little weight before their death. This happens because the Etheric material from their bodies is transferred to an astral body. Near death experiences also have this effect. Manifestation in Dimensions To function properly closer to their physical dimension, all non-physical entities must have some Etheric Matter. These entities become void of Etheric matter and return to the same dimension where they came from. This matter is only available in the physical realm and is redundant. The Silver Cord facilitates the flow and regulation of energy. It acts like an umbilical cable and ties the two parts of a body. However, it also regulates the energy flow. The projector can often see the cord and the connection between the bodies. This depends on his beliefs and his chakra system. To sustain itself in astral dimensions, the body must have energy from the body. Astral bodies that aren't stocked with energy will suffer. They will lose the ability to remember what they have seen in the astral dimension. It is important that energy flows are coordinated in order to allow the astral body to recall vivid memories and stay with you when you return to this world. Chakras: It can take many years to learn how to fully control and use your chakras. This does not mean that it is impossible to master before you experience your Out of Body Experience. With a strong energy flow, there are some basic steps that will get you through the first few stages. Learn how to control your chakra points and control your energy flow. This will allow you to change your lucid dreams, and even your astral experience. This allows you to have another life in a different dimension. You can also use it to learn and grow in each dimension. Higher Levels - Just like the astral, there are higher levels where a person can exist. These are called Adi (Anupadaka), Atmic Buddhic Mental Astral, Astral, and Mental. This level requires a lot more consciousness. Each level has some areas that lie between them. These are often called buffer zones. To fully understand this concept, consider

Earth's atmosphere to be the Astral dimension. If you wish to enter Stratosphere, which can also be considered the buffer area in this example, you will require a body specifically designed for that purpose. A jet plane is required to reach the Mental level or outerspace. You will also need a spaceship and a Mental body.

To reach the higher levels and their buffer zone requires energy. There are methods that can help you move from one dimension to the next. A fine control of the chakras is required to project energy into the higher levels. The ability to control these chakras is what allows one to produce the energy required to achieve the next level of consciousness and to become conscious. There are many techniques to help awaken awareness. These techniques can lead you to more controlled projections and higher levels of consciousness. The astral is the primary body. Other bodies such as the mind are just a part. If an individual has enough energy, they can project their astral bodies in the astral dimension. The astral bodies then project other bodies in their respective dimensions.

The ability to simultaneously experience multiple dimensions and realms at once allows one to have memories of all dimensions and can be used as a way to access many dimensions.

The most dominant memories are those which are experienced by the body with the greatest energy. You need to have a lot experience and skills in order to project your abilities into higher levels. One must be able control his chakras, and his consciousness. Although it can take time, it is possible. People have been doing this for years.

They have also written about their experiences. People have had the experience of projecting into Atmic and Buddhic levels as well as Mental and Astral. But, these two aren't among the most common. Astral Dimension: In this dimension you can observe the world as it is. They appear very real.

You can make them change as long as you give them permission. You can do whatever you like in this realm. This realm perceives time more slowly than in the physical world. It is possible to imagine stunning scenes that will appear right before your eyes. You can use your super powers to have fun. Dream pools are available in the astral dimension.

But for most people, it is not as easy as they think. It is necessary to be experienced in this area before you can have such a trip. A dream is simply a visualisation of a reality that you can't control. If your mind is strong enough and can control your subconscious, you can view anything you want in your dreams. Projecting into Virtual Reality: This is a simple way to create a personal reality for oneself. All you need is a poster that depicts natural scenery. The poster should be no larger than a standard one. But, it's okay to get a bigger version. Placing the poster on the wall will allow you to project it. You can also place a spotlight to illuminate it. Make sure there are no other lights in the room. Next, turn on the spotlight. Then, start walking slowly towards the poster. Don't stop thinking and just go. Your subconscious will see the poster as a realm, rather than a 2D one. Keep at it and soon you'll be inside the poster's realm. Then you'll not be able to tell whether it is real or artificial. This is an effective and simple way to customize your world. You can also take objects from other photographs and put them on your poster. This will make them part of the realm that you visit when you walk into it.

Chapter 2: How do you train for Astral Projection?

Training In order to be able to enter the realms of Astral there are certain training requirements you will need. 1. You must be at your best when you awaken. 2. Make sure you pay attention to everything that is going on. 3. Your body should contain some physical energy. Make your astral self project from your physical body. If you do these four things together, you can trigger an Astral Projection. Below are the exercises that can help with calming down, concentrating, and entering the state projection. 1. Relaxation. It is important to practice relaxation. If you know one, you can use it. Here's another way to relax your body. Lie down or sit down and pay attention to your feet. You can now make your feet tense, then relax them. Next, work your way up to your calves. Then move on to the thighs. Each muscle group should be targeted individually, and you can continue this until you feel totally relaxed. For trance, you need to experience deep relaxation. It is much easier to reach the astral dimension when you are in this state. 2. Meditation is about contemplation. Clearing your mind and thoughts of random thoughts is essential. When you start trying to meditate, there will be many thoughts. They will overtake you and make your attention difficult. But, you must get rid of them so that you can fully focus on projecting your astral bodies out of your physical. The best thing to do is to learn about them and solve them. Take a look at the one you are most troubled by. It is worth taking the time to reflect on it and to get a deeper understanding of it. Once you have cleared your thoughts, it is time to move on with the exercises that help clear your mind in order to focus your attention on projection. 3. Breath awareness meditation This form of meditation can help you relax and clear your mind. Here are some ways to do it. The relaxation exercise I mentioned earlier will help you relax. Take a deep breathe and let it flow through your lungs. Keep your attention on the flow of air through your lungs. Continue this practice for a while and any distractions will disappear. Because your surface mind is now preoccupied with this thought, you can think on deeper levels. 4. Surface Thoughts: Sounds can create surface thoughts. A person's voice can trigger thoughts such as "Who am I?" and "What are they saying?" These sounds should be ignored and used to improve concentration. Instead of using music to mask the sounds, it is better to listen to them than to use other types. This will enable you to master different sounds while avoiding them interfering with your concentration. 5. Concentration Concentration forms the basis of all this training. Concentration is the key to all this training. To project in the astral successfully, you will need to use all of your mental power and concentration. Concentration is essential in order to project in the astral. This is an easy way to test your concentration. Relax. Now close your eyes. You can count your breaths by taking deep, steady breaths. Keep counting your breaths. Make sure you are not thinking about anything else. The moment you allow a thought to drift away from counting your breathes, it is time to start counting from the beginning. While it is important to be able to hold your breath for at least 10 minutes, this is not enough. Even if you don't manage to reach ten, you can still improve your concentration with these exercises. Concentration Exercise-1: In a calm setting, place a lamp, preferably a torch, and gaze at it for a while. When you close your eyes, this will create an image in your brain. Focus as hard and focused as possible on this image. Focus on the image and hold it in your mind. Keep it there for as long as you can. Instead of letting it fade, make sure to use your mental power to make it grow. This is what you can call "After Image Retention". Concentration Exercise-2: To improve your concentration, you will need to look at the spot on a wall. The only thing you need to do is keep your eyes focused on the spot. It is best to just look at the spot and not think about it. It is enough to keep looking at it. If you get distracted by a thought, just let it go. This can be continued for as long you're able. Because this is an easy exercise, you can do it multiple time per day. Concentration Exercise 3 - Sit down and relax. Do not think about any other thoughts and close your eyes. Your breaths will be your focus. Imagine the air you inhale being full of life energy. You can inhale it and feel energized. Think of how the air you exhale is gray. It is full with your body's waste and negative energies.

This exercise helps you to cleanse your body and recharges your chakras. While these exercises might seem burdensome at first, once you stop thinking about things, it will become much easier to get rid of them. You'll find it very relaxing to clear your head as you go. Trance state: You will begin to feel heavier than you normally do when you let your body relax and calm your mind. This will make you feel more relaxed and will cause you to feel heavier. This is the sign that your body is entering a state called trance. The reason you feel so heavy is that your brain waves have changed due to deep relaxation. This is normal, and it's not something to worry about. It is a sign that your mind and body are fully aware, but you are actually sleeping. How to Get into a Trance. Use your breath awareness and relax exercise to calm yourself. Now, imagine that the ladder is hidden from your sight and that you don't have to. Now imagine the ladder in total darkness. Then climb it. Use your exhales to sync your movement, e.g. You can climb down a few stairs with each exhale. Your goal is to feel the impact of your falling down. If you do it right, your brain's state will change from awake to deep sleep. If you feel you are in the "trance" state (i.e. When you feel heavy, you can stop fantasizing about the ladder climbing. The ladder can be viewed as a metaphor for your life, or you could think of yourself like a feather. It is designed to create a falling effect that helps you get into a trance state. It will be a different feeling to everything when you are in the state of trance. It becomes more peaceful and you feel as though you are in another dimension. The body can feel as if it is vibrating slow and things become blurred. Deep Trance There's a range of levels of deep trance. What level you attain depends on how relaxed and committed you are. The beta level is when your consciousness is awake. Alpha is when your sleep is asleep. However, theta refers to deep sleep. You must keep working out for longer periods to reach this level. Projection is not difficult even when you are in alpha-level trance. Deep trance has certain symptoms that you can look out for to determine if you are there. * It feels like you're losing your heat. * It's as if everything is happening at a slower speed than usual. * You feel detached from your body. * Your body is unable or unwilling to move. Paralysis. Although you may feel some of these symptoms while in alpha, you won't be capable of recognizing them if you are deep in trance. At the moment, you will know that deep sleep is in your body. Additionally, it will take effort to get there. The best thing about this is that you don't have worry about it. You can still get out of discomfort any time you feel it. Feeling uneasy? Move one of your fingers or toes. After that, you can concentrate your energy on moving other parts of your body. This will help you get out of sleep. Energy Body Expanding When someone first enters a state of trance, he loses control of his body and starts vibrating everywhere. After that, the body seems to expand. These symptoms can indicate that your body is in a normal sleep pattern. You can actually see your energy body expanding to hold more energy. This is called energy body extension. Trance Familiarity. It is simple to get out of a trance state. Many people are unfamiliar with the phenomenon and think they have initiated their astral realm. Because this is false, many people end up feeling unstable while in trance. The ability to maintain a stable mental and physical state in a trance will allow him to continue it for longer times. When they first enter this state, they quickly get excited and attempt to reach astral as fast as possible. It can ruin a great opportunity because of their increased excitement. People who first enter this state will find it difficult to remain calm and stable. You should maintain your concentration, and become familiar with the state in order to feel it. Keep these tips in mind: * Trance does not help you understand the energy and chakra. It is not something you should do. This is the best place to go to get into this state. Once you get into a trance, your body will appear as if it is floating in space. To be able to control your movement in the astral dimension, your arms will need to be extended and your legs will need to be lifted slowly. It is not necessary to move your body muscles in order to achieve this. Simply focus on the sensations in your astral body, and you can feel your arms and legs. Tactile Image A person is able perceive the presence and parts of his body. Tactile Imaging refers to the ability to feel your body's parts and determine their distance from you. If you want to become aware of your physical body and its parts, you should pretend you will touch your imaginary body parts using your imaginary hands. You don't have the ability to move or attempt to move your arm and hand muscles. Hold your eyes closed, and place your hands on your palms. As you move your arms, twist your wrists, turn your hands, and keep your focus on the position of your hands, try to imagine them. You can do the same thing with different parts of your body. Feel the sensation through the concentrating power in your mind. This will allow your mind to be fully focused on the area that you feel the most comfortable touching. It will also enable you to use the power of the mind to move your imaginary world hard. You can then move your awareness from one body part to another, and use this to aid you in your projections practices. This is a great way to practice projections. You don't even need to hold an image of any body parts. All you have to do is pretend to feel your body moving and touching others. Blind people, especially those born blind have limited visualization abilities, but have an awareness. They are aware of the parts of their bodies just like someone who has sight, even if his eyes are closed. However, projection techniques rely on visualization, which can make it difficult for blind people with vision impairment to use these techniques. The tactile imaging technique mentioned above is useful both for those who are blind and for those who can see.

Chapter 3: Basic Energy Works

The chakra points of the body are responsible for the functioning of energy. There are seven major chakra points within the body. They regulate the flow of spiritual and physical energies throughout the body. Stable chakra regulation is important for normal and proper functioning of the body. These are the names of the seven chakra points: * Root Chakra* Spleen Chakra* Solar Plexus Chakra* Heart Chakra* Heart Chakra* Heart Chakra* Heart Chakra* Heart Chakra* Heart Chakra* Heart Chakra* Heart Chacra * Throat Chakra* Thoroat Chakra* Crown Chakra. Chakras are organs in your body that aren't physically active but which play an important part in the energy flow throughout your body. They are about the size of a small palm and are sometimes drawn in the shape a sphere. They receive energy from the Earth or the universe and turn it into energy circulation. The energy that unites the universe is the subtle energy that chakras draw out of the universe. It is the energy in the universe. A person can tap into the vast field of energy by concentrating on a single thing and focusing inwardly with willpower. This can then be used for different purposes. The entire system of chakras is complex because there are more than 300. The major chakras are the seven mentioned above. Each one plays a significant role in our lives. Some chakra points extend outside the body. The complete diagram of all chakras points can be found here. This chart has been in existence for many centuries. You can't expect any psychic ability to be produced without control over the chakra points. There are many different methods to stimulate the chakras. All psychic effects, regardless of how they are perceived, are directly connected to chakra stimulation. Some people trust spiritual entities to enhance their psychic abilities. Others rely on their faith. If a person is able control his chakras, he can access some psychic abilities. These steps can be used to raise your energy. First, let go of all thoughts. Now, you can relax by sitting down. To achieve this, breathe awareness exercises can be used. You can now imagine there is energy beneath your feet. Without moving, you can use your hands and fingers to reach the energy. You should feel like your palms are holding the energy and your body is pulling it. To speed up this process, you can use breath awareness to increase the amount of energy that is collected in your lungs. Continue this process for a few more minutes. Keep in mind that your exercise is still giving physical energy, even if no visible results are observed. This will allow you to draw more energy from the exercises if you keep working on the chakra points. The natural path of energy is from the feet to your root chakra. It then flows into the stream of the energy. This stream of energy can be used as energy to your mental body, astral body and other subtle organs. When you project back into the physical realm, you will be able to recall information from that level. Chakra Stimulation Chakras, their stimulation, is a huge subject. There are many different methods you can use to stimulate your chakra. Dedication and commitment are key. However, experience is important.

For beginners, you can begin with a few simple exercises and then work your way up. Opening a Chakra Point: You will need your imagination to open a chakra. It is like opening a packet of snacks. Focus on your imaginary hands and use them to find the spot where the chakra point is. It is important to remember that chakras don't exist in physical form. If you want to stimulate them, then you need to use something that isn't physical like the one here. Start at the root when trying to stimulate each of the seven chakras. It can be opened using the procedure described above. Next, you can try to draw planet-energy from your feet. This chakra point can also be drawn energy by using breath awareness. Repeat the process for the root chakra five to seven additional times. You can then move on the Spleen. During stimulation of the Spleen's energy, you must draw it again from your feet. Next, let the energy flow through the root and into its Spleen. Continue doing this five to seven times more. Use the imaginary hands to practice opening it. The same way, you can open your chakra points directly from your feet. You should always begin with the root chakra. This is because it acts as a gateway to energy for the next chakras. It is recommended to give your root your full concentration and stimulate it fully when you first start working with your chakra systems. It is possible to not notice any significant changes in your chakra points for several months. However, this doesn't mean that you should worry. Your internal chakra points will keep growing and developing even after you stop working on them. Chakra Sensations Training and concentration exercises will have an effect on how your chakra points feel. These factors include your willpower and relaxation skills. Sometimes, you might sense warmth. Other sensations include a feeling like you are getting a little dizziness, a slight pressure buildup and a moving sensation. These sensations can be felt in one or multiple places at once. In the later stages, you may feel a slight pulsing sensation within your body. Each chakra point has its own sensation. Psychic Abilities When you start working on chakras, you'll soon discover that you have psychic talents.

This natural effect is due to chakra stimulations. You can read more about this in literature that is related to chakras or psychic abilities. For the best results, practice daily. Practice breathing exercises, meditation, and relaxation will only improve if you do them regularly. It's easier to improve your practice the more you do it. You don't need special equipment or a specific environment to make this work. How long does it all take? The process can seem daunting to beginners, so they continue asking questions. There is no time limit. Some people will notice results within weeks while others might see them over months or years. It all depends upon the individual's natural skills and how they adapt to a particular practice. It is only possible to discover the answer by trying.

Chapter 4: Using the Astral Rope Method

Chapter 4: Astral Rope Technique. The technique of using an "astral rope" to project into another dimension is a common one. An astralrope is a rope suspended from the ceiling. It is used to force your astral body to release its physical counterpart by applying enough pressure. You should remember that this rope is imaginary and not real. This method is more effective than any other astral projection methods. While they work, the sub-body can also be pressed out using indirect methods. However, their effect is not limited to that particular area. Some of these methods are effective on the whole body and others on just a part. These methods are great for projecting the body. However, some of them may prove difficult to envision, especially for those who are new to it. Astral Rope allows you to visualize yourself pulling on a rope and using it for support. This technique allows a person to combine his mental and conscious powers to pull this off. For such projections, there are many clever options. Some use pressure to do this, while others use a passive approach. Meditation is often a practice that allows you to think you are doing something. Concentration can lead to a greater disconnect from your surroundings. This helps reduce brain activity, and shifts the brain waves pattern to the desired state. This state allows one to access other realms through any activity that helps him be more aware of his deeper self. People often make the mistake to apply pressure to their subtle body in a passive fashion. There is nothing wrong in this, but it is important to remember that the direction they are trying push the astral body in can often be wrong. People will try to focus their attention on a subtle, departed body. They then attempt to transfer their consciousness into that body by closing their eyes. This is a complicated approach that has a low success rate, especially for beginners. People fail to see the value of this knowledge and are often unable to achieve their goals. While passive techniques for pressing on the subtle bodies are effective, it takes time. They require a lot of time to begin working, as they exert pressure on many parts of the body. The rope technique offers the advantage that it makes use of all your resources and makes maximum use to your mental faculties to make your projections go faster. This is where motivation is crucial. If you lack motivation, it will be difficult to project any type of image. This is because projection depends on your mind power. Motivation comes from motivation. How to Get the Feel of Rope. To get the feel of a imaginary rope, use a simple tactile tool. You can hang a ribbon on the ceiling of your bedroom. If you reach out to touch it, it will be visible. Then, touch it frequently with your fingers so you are familiar with the position of the ribbon in your bedroom. This will assist you in positioning the imaginary rope. The thought form of the rope will continue developing in the astral realm. When you reach out and grab the rope, you'll know where it is. Also, remember that you will be climbing up the imaginary rope using your imagination. This isn't the right way to think about climbing a rope. This technique can help you shift the point of consciousness. As your body changes due to your climbing, this technique is beneficial. Active Chakra Remember that you should imagine the rope at a natural angle so it is easy to climb. There are two ways to imagine the rope. There are two possible angles. One is to imagine the rope ending at your eyebrow chakra. The other is to imagine it ending at the heart chakra. If your brow chakra is active, you might imagine the rope hanging from your head. Otherwise, you could imagine the rope reaching your chest. You can increase your chances of projection by moving the point of extraction towards the chakra point with more energetic. It is important that the rope be angled so that it can be climbed easily and naturally. It will be difficult to imagine climbing the rope if it isn't. Are You Ready to Try Projecting Right Now? Now that you've read about many exercises to help you project, the question is whether you're ready to actually try it. The majority of these training exercises are meant to help you prepare for projecting, but not for the actual task. Sometimes these exercises may leave you with less mental energy than you need for projection. If this happens, you might not be able or willing to do any projections. Remember that you cannot train and project simultaneously. Do your first training to increase energy, chakra control, energy accumulation and your body's energy. Only then can you start thinking about how to project. Training is designed to help you project more consciously. No matter what training method or what type of training, success is what matters. Training exercises help you to relax, stop worrying about the future and focus. The exercise using imaginary hands is meant to help you learn MBA. Mobile bodily awareness, and you can move on to the next stages once you have mastered this technique. Your chakra control is designed to regulate and control energy that you have created through different energy raising exercises. Exercises to induce a state or trance can help you to get closer to the goal of projection. When to do the Exercises. Although these exercises are not necessary for projection, they can be useful. As we mentioned, it is important to make a habit out of practicing these basic exercises on a daily base. Furthermore, you should become comfortable using Imaginary Händes. You should also perform other more demanding exercises as often as you have the time, but not less than once per week. Your Projection Sequence. There is no standard or prescribed sequence. People work in different ways. You will need to decide the sequence. But there is a basic sequence you can follow until it becomes more comfortable for you. Relaxation techniques used to fully relax * Clear your mind by using breath awareness. Use the mental falling method or any other technique to get into a state that is similar to trance. * Stimulate your chakras. * Project out with the Rope technique. Either enter trance to stimulate chakras or first work on them. It all depends on your personal nature. The right sequence will be determined based on that. Stimulation of chakras can lead to trance states for some people. For beginners, ROPE for

Projection ROPE can be used to project. This method is great for those who are not good at concentration and meditation. You can make a normal projection into astral dimension by using rope method. Your ability to control the energy level and length of your projection into that dimension determines how long it lasts. Use this technique to relax until there are no worries and you are completely settled.

* Now, imagine your hands climbing on the rope. This is an experience of sensation. You don't need to visualize or use your hands. You must feel the sensation of gripping the rope and climbing on it with your imaginary hand. You will lose your concentration if you visualize the rope and start thinking about it. Even if it is difficult to concentrate, it will still take energy from your body. As you climb higher, you may feel dizziness. This is caused by the pressure on your subtle, spiritual body. Very important

Note. * You must keep track of the exact event that caused this dizziness. This feeling can be described as progress. You should strive to feel it every time that you do this exercise. * If you want to project into an astral domain, avoid any feelings. You can focus on climbing the rope. But, you should also be relaxed. * Never stop climbing the rope if your body starts to feel heavy or vibrating. You must keep climbing until your body is out of control. How to deal with vibrations: At some point during the process you will feel vibrations in your body. You don't need worry or be concerned about these vibrations. They are an energy movement across your entire chakra system. If you find these vibrations disturbing, you should learn to ignore them. If you keep them from projecting, it will be difficult for you to focus. Concentrating more on these exercises will help you improve your concentration. The foundation of rope projection is the ability to imagine hands that move through your body. Even though it is not necessary, it is important as it will help to overcome many obstacles. The best thing is that it cuts down the time it takes to successfully project. You can learn this skill but your efficiency will increase dramatically if it is a part of your repertoire. If you can climb the rope without being distracted, you will soon enter a state where you can trance. That will open your chakra points. Next are the vibrations. After that you will experience your first projected. The process is quick and easy for beginners. They are afraid it will take too much time and be difficult to understand. But once you get used, you will appreciate the efficiency and speed of this process. Because it's fast, you save a lot on mental energy which can be used later in your astral domain to enhance your experience and help you remember when you wake. Some other methods require you learn all skills before your can start projecting into other dimensions. With this method, you just need to have good concentration. Rope technique can be used if you have the ability to focus and execute mental actions. Do not ignore the technique if it isn't working for you. Instead, conduct a stepwise check to determine the source of the problem. Then, use the training exercises that you've learned to resolve it. A Rope variation With a few modifications one can use a variant of ROPE. This variation lets you complete the whole sequence but not project into the astral. You can pause the entire sequence when you reach the stage where you will need to close the chakras. Grab something to drink or eat. Get up, then lie down or take a seat in your chair. Next, start climbing the rope. How Rope Works Mechanics This article will give you a quick explanation of how this incredible method triggers astral projection. Clearing

Your Mind: Once you start climbing the rope your mind will be completely clear and focus on that process. Brain Wave Activity. Your brain's activity is reduced when you have no other thoughts, and your body feels direct pressure. Deep Relaxation: The brain's activity is at its lowest level, allowing the body to relax to a deeper level. Trance: A state when the body is in a relaxed state, and the brain is not performing any activity, it is called trance. The Chakras. When the astral body is under constant pressure, it opens the chakras and stimulates them. Vibrations - Energy flows through all chakra points if they are open. When this happens, it means that an energy body in expanded state is exerting pressure on the chakras. This creates vibrations in the body. Separation is caused by continuous pressure on the aura body. If the person is in a vibrational state, the aura is forced out of their physical bodies and projected into the astral dimension. The projection reflex can be avoided by pressingurizing the astral organ when you are about for it to project. This allows you to control the projection and how it happens, instead of letting your body do the rest. This will enable you to project in any direction and in any rope. How Long is it before You Can Project? A good project can be completed in 15 minutes if one is focused. If you are good enough you can complete it in ten minutes. Rope, as I have repeatedly stated, optimizes your energy. It makes use of all of it in one go and not slowly over time. The other thing to keep in mind is that you should be able succeed in between 15 and 20 minutes. If you don't succeed, you can take a break from the rope and start over again. It is impossible to appreciate and fully comprehend the value of this method unless you have tried it. Also, it is worth trying out other methods so you can compare them with

Rope. Rope as experienced by a person. There are many people that have tried other techniques with success, but one tried the Rope method. He claims that the idea of astral projection with rope came to his mind while he was just about to go to sleep. He wasn't able to do specific exercises because he was ready for sleep. He immediately started to pull the rope and used his imaginary hands as his guide. The first symptoms of the early stages appeared as soon he began. He mentioned feeling dizziness as well as tickling sensations throughout his body and bones. As it is against the rules to think and feel anything, he concentrated all his attention on climbing up the rope. This was putting tremendous pressure on his subtle astral body. Soon the upper astral organs began to grow out of the body and go higher up the rope. He pulled and soon experienced a deep trance. After losing control over his physical body, he felt strong vibrations. He continued to pull on the rope, and within a matter of minutes, was out of his own physical body. According to him, he projected before using other methods. However, this project was quite different because it involved a reflex. Although the astral body naturally leaves the physical, in this case he was free to leave the body. He began to floate in the air of his bedroom and tried to get out of the wall. There was no resistance, but instead of ending in the lounge behind the wall he ended at a completely new place. One house had a thatched roofing, just like the ones from the past. A fence was visible to the side and there was a small lake. The experience didn't seem to make sense at first. The boredom soon became a constant companion so he began to look at his hands and saw that they were slowly melting away. Soon, his fingers began losing their shape. He wanted them all to grow back, so he started seeing the results. But as soon as it was over, they began melting back. He learned that fingers only grow as long he keeps his eyes on the growth. At that moment, he realized that the entire world that he was in was actually an image that hangs on his wall. This is the exact spot where he tried floating out to the lounge. The house, the lake, and even the sunlight were part of this drawing. This roughly explained melting. After realizing that, he realized there wasn't much more. He tried to get his physical body back by moving his eyes or lips. This was enough to stop his projection and wake him up. After being fully awakened, he began to write down his first rope projection. He then tried again with the same experiment, and within minutes was able to project once more. He attempted to move closer to the painting again and noticed that it began to grow. He started moving closer to it and noticed that it was getting larger. He decided to go back into it just in case. The world seemed so real that he felt like he was actually there. The environment smelled and felt like air, and everything seemed totally real. Because he had already been in the world, he was able to return to it and write down everything. Remembering It The problem that most people face with any Out-of-Body-Experience is that even though they try to remember it, it is just keeps fading away and in the end, they are just left with the memory of it happening sometimes. This problem can be solved. Just as you wake up, take the time to remember everything you have experienced. It's a good idea for you to keep a journal. You should also dedicate a few minutes every morning to write down any memories. You'll be stimulating your dream memory, and general memory. You can ask yourself things such as "Was someone talking to me?" or "Was there a trip?" or "I was in this place" etc. This will help you bring back bits of your memories. You can create all the phrases that you need to help with memory and recalling. Once you have the one end of a memory, you will be able to locate other parts. Keep a journal. This is not a suggestion, but a recommendation. Like dreams, they may be completely remembered at first, but then you begin to lose parts until they disappear completely. Therefore, it is recommended that you keep an account. Stuck during Projection? Projection can sometimes cause an astral body part to become stuck. This happens when the head is at the end. While it may be possible to climb higher in some cases, this can lead to discomfort and even actual pain. Make sure your chakra points are stimulated to help you cope. Be mindful of your health, and eat healthy. You should start your projecting exercises after your meal has finished. This will ensure that there isn't too much digestion interfering in your projecting. If the problem is chakra-related, identify the area. Once you have pinpointed the chakra causing problems, perform the appropriate exercises to regulate the flow energy through that chakra. You must stabilize it first for a successful projection and for better health.

Chapter 5: Astral Projection; The Basics

We'll be looking at simple exercises that can be done by anyone to attain Astral Projection. Before we start, we'll review some basic terms and principles to help you apply these techniques.

How and when to practice astral projection

Astral Projection can be best achieved when we sleep. However, it should not to be confused with vivid dreams or lucid dreaming. These are difficult to achieve without years of practice and sometimes with great sacrifice. In some traditions, such Eastern religions as Buddhism, monks are known to induce trance states. This requires meditation and years of practice. Additionally, it is a time-consuming process that can be difficult to live with in the real world. For most people, practicing Astral Projection while sleeping is the best and easiest method. Astral Projection could be described as an altered state of consciousness. In a sense, Astral Projection is when we go to sleep and, especially, when we dream, it's when we reach another level of knowledge. For most people, this is the best and easiest time to practice Astral Projection.

Astral Projection is an approach to separating the Astral or spirit body from the body. Many techniques allow you to visualize the two bodies and "split" them. This section focuses on this principle. However, it offers many different methods to achieve the same goal. Different techniques work well for most people. Try several different methods to determine what works best. Anyone can learn Astral Projecting, but it does require patience and practice. Some people may be concerned that Astral Projection will make it more difficult or leave you unable connect with your body. This is false. It's important to understand, at least for now, that Astral Projection is intrinsically connected to our physical and Astral bodies. You can't disconnect them or lose your way to either.

Sleep Paralysis

It is an average effect that we experience when we are asleep. Our brains block the signals our body receives to respond to the external world. This is to protect our bodies from harm while we are dreaming. The brain interprets dream images as real and does NOT distinguish between conscious and sleep experiences. The brain causes paralysis, which prevents us from jumping, running, or doing any other type of physical activity in response to "external stimulusi." While we may sense the difference in our dreams, we do not make the movements or actions that result in the goal. Astral Projection is used to induce sleep paralysis. Astral Projection gives us the opportunity to experience the real world. It allows us to travel through the Astral plane to different parts in the physical world. However our perceptions can still impact our physical body.

The Hypnagogic Status

This is the condition we find ourselves in just before sleeping, at the border of conscious perception and unconscious consciousness. This is where the brain disconnects our physical responses. It is often called sleep paralysis. It's essential to be able to control this condition. This is something that can take practice but most people will soon master.

Relaxation and Meditation

Most people are familiar with techniques to achieve these ends. These techniques can be very useful when practicing Astral Projection. Astral Projection requires that the body and mind relax completely. The first step in Astral Projection is to understand how to get there. Without this, it's likely that you won't see much success. This does not require that you learn how to clear the mind. Instead, it requires learning how to live in the moment.

Vibration

This refers to a sensation you will feel when your Astral bodies begins to make their presence known. The sensation can be described as a slight tingling sensation that spreads throughout your body. You might also feel your body "floating". This is sometimes called "Astral Body Lifting". It's not unpleasant, and your body will often feel filled with light energy and energy.

Astral Projection Techniques

Separation

This is a simple exercise to help you separate your Astral and Physical bodies. You must travel within the confines of the room you are in. Before you start, select a point within the room. This could be an object, a feature, such as a bookcase, bookshelf, drawers, or corner. You can feel the objects and areas around it, as well as absorb the "sense of being there".

Relax now and get into a comfortable posture. You can now relax by closing your eyes. Now, focus on what is dark and how you are breathing. In this state, you can begin to see the object you have "learned." After focusing on the object for a few second, move on to the darkness in your front.

This process should be repeated until you feel like you are in a vibrational state. You will feel complete separation from your body shortly after reaching this state.

The Rope

Robert Bruce, a mystic, popularized this Projection technique. It is simple and often very efficient. After you are calm, relaxed, and have entered the zone between waking/sleeping, visualize a rope hanging over you. Imagine your eyes closed with your body relaxed. Now imagine reaching for the rope. Imagine climbing the rope. What feelings would you have? How would your muscles tense and what weight your body would bear. For real, don't tense muscles. Continue to climb mentally and speed up your progress. Your vibrations should be quite rapid and you will continue to accelerate your ascent until separation.

Exhaust Yourself

The mind should be alert and the body must be exhausted in order to seperate the Astral and Physical bodies. Get as active as you possibly can during the day. Get out for a walk, run, or stay active until the late hours. You can keep your mind active by reading or writing and playing games that require a lot of mental activity, such as chess. It is possible to fall into deep sleep. Instead, you can focus on the feeling of going to bed and let your body "fall away." Once you enter a hypnagogic stage, you will begin to feel the vibrations. As the hypnagogic state develops, imagine getting up and moving around. Your Astral body will begin to separate and fall asleep.

Falling Awake

This technique can either be used in the morning or at night. You can simply relax when you awaken in the morning. Keep your eyes closed, and you will force sleep to return. The Astral body will then be forced to awaken from a vibrational state. This can be a very quick technique and extremely useful, but you will need to practice it. The trick is not to miss the Hypnagogic stage as it develops. Instead, train your Astral Body "jump away" at this point. As soon as you start to drift off at night, you should practice this. Let your brain think that you are going to fall asleep but then pull your Astral body from the physical.

Keep your eyes on the Familiar

To reach deep relaxation, you can focus your attention on an everyday object that is familiar to you. An excellent choice is something that you don't think about but are familiar with. A smartphone, keys for your car or house, or even your phone, are all good examples. Visualize how the object feels inside your hand. Think about the weight texture, feel and overall feeling of the object. As the visualization gets more detailed, you'll notice that your entire Astral Body vibrates at a rate where you can just slip into it. This will allow you to achieve Projection.

Tunnel Vision

An easy and accessible visualization for Projection is to see a dark tunnel with an end light. You can imagine yourself flying through the tunnel as you continue to visualize. The vibrational state will start to manifest. You may experience sounds and visions in this state, but these should be ignored. Keep your eyes on the light and move towards it. As soon as you enter it, both your Astral body and physical body will split.

The Thirst Technique

Sylvan Mulloon, an early pioneer for Astral travel as well as altered states of awareness, invented this technique. This technique should not be used often and should only be used by people who are in good physical health. Although the benefits are great, they don't make good long-term decisions for your health. Even those who are in good health may want to avoid it. Just avoid drinking liquids for several hours prior to going to sleep. Muldoon advocated salty foods to increase thirst. This isn't a sensible move for health. You will feel intense thirst if you eat salty foods before you go to sleep. You should keep it out of reach. When you start to fall asleep, concentrate on this water. It would be great to reach for it and then take a long, deep breath. This is not a time to act physically. However, keep the visualization secure and at the forefront. As you go to bed, the desire for water and the view should become a compelling urge in your body. This will create separation between your Astral bodies and your physical ones.

Chapter 6: Near Death Experience

Additionally, near-death experiences do not have to be limited to people of religious or spiritual faith. People of all walks and religions have reported OOBE. Near-death experiences don't seem to discriminate between devout Christians and confirmed atheists.

All history has been filled with near-death events, a type of OOBE. These events are now more frequent thanks to modern science and medicine. Modern medical techniques make "death" less random and many people can be "brought home" from the dead. Near-death has become more common. People who have experienced near-death or OOBE often report seeing themselves from above.

Many aspects of these reports are varied, but many include the sensation, sight, or feeling of moving towards light, or of meeting beings or relatives who died. For those who report back on an event, it is often that someone has spoken to them and told them that they're not ready. In many cases there is a remarkable consistency in these reports. Although scientists and doctors are skeptical of the claims, some medics have taken precautions to test it. They placed objects high up in a darkened room so that no one could see them, not even a patient who was prone or dead. The results showed that our existence may go beyond physical perceptions.

Possibility not to wake up

People ask the question "Can I kill myself while projecting?" This is a common question. However, it is much more complicated than that. First let's examine the "yes". Anybody can die while projecting. This means that even if your home burns down in the middle of the night, or if there is an earthquake, you can still die. The chance that your physical bodies will not be aware of any danger is very low. Although they may be separate, Astral and Physical bodies can still work together. The link that links them will not be broken, and your Astral body's ability to return to normal will be impeded by physical danger. Science can't even imagine the speed at which this will happen. If your Astral presence is threatened, your physical body "calls" your Astral bodies back to it. Astral travel can happen over infinite distances in just seconds, and the return journey takes only seconds.

We're referring to the "no" part of the answer. It is whether you or others can kill you on Astral Plane. Some believe that if it were possible, then the individual would not be able to tell us. However, they would be able to communicate with us (on the Astral level) and it is not a matter that comes up. To be able to die on this plane, the cord that ties you to your physical body must be removed. This cord cannot be cut using psychic methods. In difficult situations, you can easily call upon the protection of the Astral Master (including Christ) or your spirit guides. The help and protection you need will be offered to you without any fear, favor, or judgment. It is never withheld, and if you ever feel genuine concern about the Astral Plane's existence, try to focus on the idea of requiring assistance, visualize white, healing lights, and work towards it.

Lost or Stalled

Some people fear that they might lose their way once they have left their body. This will not occur. It is possible to be delayed while on your trip, but it will not happen. The best analogy you can use is to imagine that you are travelling abroad. It may take you longer to get home than you anticipated, but you'll always be able find your home when you return. The connection between your physical and spiritual bodies is too strong for you to lose. As with the previous issues, you can rely on spirit guides and ascended souls for guidance back to your home. Projection is a practice that will minimize any delay. As you practice Projection regularly, you'll notice delays disappear.

Are Near-Death Experiencings a Type or Astral Projection?

Yes. The difference between Astral Projection or a near death experience is that the former are voluntary. Astral Projection can be used for spiritual growth or fun. Near-death experiences are when a person is actually going through the process of death. The spirit, or the life force of the soul, separates from the body to cross over and begin the journey from death to life. It is often a long, dark hallway that leads to a white light. This white light is where death occurs. Sometimes they may see their final moments before death, and even take stock of their life. The person's astral life is saved. He returns to his body from the astral realm. The experience is near death and the person isn't in control.

Demonic Possession

This is a very real fear. There will be "Demons", at some time in your journey. They are negative energies. These are souls trapped in Astral Plane. They will seek out ways to get back on the physical plane, and they may consider you a short-cut. They can be stopped by being careful. For those who have not yet incarnated on Earth, you can call upon spirits for assistance. Your spirit guides will also be available to assist you. Remember to imagine you are in a lighter place. You will find yourself moving towards it quickly.

Always have your back. If you give your permission, no negative entity or person can possess your spirit or physical body. They may try to convince you or trick you, but again, seek the help of more powerful and ascended beings. If you meet less-pleasant entities while you prepare to enter the physical body again, or are waiting in the area where your physical anatomy lies, tell them that you will be leaving. Many people find this difficult to believe. However, "demons", are simply spirits who are not ready to re-incarnate. Their place is not in this world, it is yours. Tell them this and tell them it's time for them to move on. They may appear unwilling to go, but they are unable to argue with the fact that it is time for them to leave.

When is the Best Time for Astral Projects?

It is very important not to astralproject at night or near your bedtime. It is simply too dangerous to go to sleep and miss out on the experience. Although it might seem obvious that it would be most relaxing right before bedtime, evidence suggests that this is not true. People report it being the easiest because it's the closest to hypnagogic states and you're still getting up. But, it may not be possible for everyone due to work or family commitments. You can astral projection whenever you have the space and time. It doesn't really matter if someone else supports it or criticizes it.

Chapter 7: Astral body

Astral body also known as "a fluid organ" It seems unlikely. The ether is mysterious and can be found everywhere. According to science, the ether is the first element in all matter. He alone is unable to create matter. Atoms of many elements contain negative electric charge, or electrons. These charges revolve around positive nuclei. Astral matter is also affected by the same structure. The only difference is the fact that astral matter has atoms/molecules infinitely smaller and vibrate with a higher frequency than physical matter. These vibrations are tuned into the senses of an astral body. Accordingly, the astral thing for astral sense organs can be as real as the physical thing for physical sense organs. Modern science can confirm the wisdom of Pythagoras. He taught twenty-five hundred years ago that matter is composed only of three elements. They are substance, motion and numbers. The "movement", which refers to electricity, is correlated to the number atoms that vibrate and the number molecule bits. This is Dr. Landler's perspective on the astral bodies.

Although the exact composition and function of the astral body are not known yet, many occultists believe it will be solved in the near future. This cannot be done in the lab. It is impossible to determine the nature of an entire body with a single projector.

The Physical Plane

In reality, Astral Projection will only take you as far as your physical body. Sound boring? Surprised? This experience is both fascinating, and it can also be frightening. Your abilities at first will be limited to what is within your immediate vicinity. Don't let this discourage you. In some ways it acts as a safety blanket for our physical and Astral bodies. Projection uses a lot energy. This energy is both psychic as well as physical. Projection can cause you to feel physically tired.

You can take your time building your strength. Start by simply exploring your immediate surroundings. This will change the way you see the world. Remember that most animals sense you and are sensitive to the spirit world.

People who form strong bonds may sense your presence even if they don't have the same psychic abilities. This might be subtle and not something they mention. However, it's important to know that Astral travel can be a strange, unsettling experience for you as well as those around you. While it might be nice to learn how to Astral contact loved ones, and to reassure yourself that they're safe and sound, it's often more respectful and appropriate to use the physical body to call.

Projection is a skill that will help you travel fartherin your neighborhood and beyond. Visit places you are familiar with to help you develop your skills. It will also make you more adept at psychic energy and the technique. This is your Astral body's workout. By practicing often, visiting places you're familiar with, your Astral body's abilities will be enhanced. As you continue to do this, you will notice that you begin to feel less tired when projecting. Astral bodies will depend on their strength for energy, projection, and other functions. Astral Projection will make you feel physically energized and spiritual energy will "cross-over" to the rest of your body over time.

Opening your Physical Mind to All the Possibilities

It is common for us to dream about what it would feel like to travel around the globe, across the universe and through time. It would be fascinating to see history as it was, or grandma at her best. We decide to stop daydreaming. What if you were told that anyone can astral project with training? You can. This isn't just for those with years of meditation in the woods on rocks. You have a soul, you have a spirit. It's up to you to let go of your spirit and allow it to run wild! You don't have to be a stranger to astral travel. It is possible, and you will. This is exactly what this book is about. We will help you get started. You'll be taking yourself to extraordinary places in both space and time. You can travel anywhere, see any person or anything. Astral Projection will open your eyes and mind to new possibilities, and more importantly, it will liberate your soul.

You probably experienced astral Projection before you realized it. It could be as a blissful daydream, or as a standard dream in your bed. The vividness of the experience would make you believe it was real. You could feel and smell the surroundings, as well as control all aspects of what was going on. You might have been traveling with someone else or communicating with the dead. They may appear to be well and offer well-being messages. What is Lucid Dreaming, you ask? Perhaps. This topic will receive more attention. Different people may experience astral travel and/or astral projection differently. However, they can still be intentionally identical. Imagine if you were told that some of those experiences were real.

Would You Believe What We Have to Say?

Most people see the soul as an entity separate from the body. It seems like a natural conclusion. This acknowledgement seems to be a common practice in many cultures. It is usually done at wakes and funerals. Then suddenly, it becomes a concern about where the soul has gone. It manifests in the comforting of the bereaved through statements such as, "They are at a better spot, this body is just another shell." The bereaved can agree to this statement without additional thought. The soul has a temporary home within our bodies. This is when it seems easy to everyone.

As third-dimensional physical beings, our tendency is to think in concrete terms about ourselves. We become lost in the physical world. We become what the mirror shows us, the sum of all the flesh and bone that we have. Many people view the soul as something that flies after losing our physicality. Most people can accept the fact that the soul has gone to another place after physical death. They don't think twice about the possibility that the consciousness or spirit may continue to thrive in another body. It is just that simple. The soul is now on a learning adventure at the next level. And boy, howdy, we wish it's a well-equipped classroom.

Recognizing the widespread acceptance that our beings have a dual nature, the spiritual as well as the physical, it is time to let go of your obsession with the material realm and to change your basic instincts. Even though you may have been there before reading this book, the fact that it was there helps to reinforce the idea. We encourage people to consider themselves not as a human body with a soul, rather than as a human body with a soul. The soul is eternal and the body is transient. Your hand is not a glove that holds a handle; your hand is a glove that holds a handle. Although it may seem simple and not difficult, some find it challenging to do. We humans have been raised to be obsessed by the physical world our whole lives. It is so important. We are very concerned about our homes, clothes, and cars. Homo sapiens has a tendency to be preoccupied by our bodies and personal belongings.

Astral projection N, also called astral travel or astral projection (we use both interchangeably)gives us a glimpse into the infinite beyond what we can see with our three-dimensional physical eyes. Abraham Maslow has a hierarchy of needs which lists that we all need water, air, and a safe place to stand. Maslow said in psychology that as physical beings, we need physiological items. Accepting yourself as a soul/spirit allows you to let go of your mind's limitations and excess weight. The spirit is free and able to explore the vast universe without the limitations of the physical world. This is the part which starts to discourage people from jumping.

Chapter 8: Vibrations

Vibrations: These are physical manifestations of an out-of body experience. However, there are significant psychological events that help the body prepare for its spiritual travel component.

The most obvious sign is movement. Movements are not the same as physical changes. They are internal actions. These vibrations, also known as vibrations, can be felt all over your body. This is believed to be the most defining sign of astral projection without any physical response.

It is possible that Earth's ghosts are a part of this thought process. Oceans are filled with the wreckage of planes and sunken vessels of ships that have been lost; people have been living there for thousands. Everything is energy. It has the potential to retain the vibrations of the past. Spirits don't have to go through a horrible death to "return". Perhaps the heavens could be the new resting area for weary astral travelers in between visits?

Anyone can make false claims about seeing or talking to spirits. This will bring down credibility for all involved in paranormal and astral travel. They also have the ability of claiming if a place they visit is haunted, active, or both. How often do living creatures take the time, in silence, to meditate and allow themselves to reach the fourth dimension? Many. This is despite our belief in the paranormal entertainment show. It's not a good practice to shout "Hey!" when you enter. My time is valuable. Show yourself and say something before your stomach turns! That is rude and disrespectful, no matter how you are living or dead.

It is possible to travel to other dimensions if you just focus your efforts. Focus your thoughts on raising your vibrational frequency so that you can travel to higher dimensions. You can also use affirmations. Mentally state, "I now reach a higher dimension." Ask your guide to take to you the next dimension.

You might feel like you're going through a tunnel to get to the higher dimension. You should be calm as this can feel intense. After travelling to higher dimensions, it is possible to need to raise your vibratory frequency.

The dizziness, another psychosomatic sign, supports the notion of astral travel. The sensation of falling, flying, and being suspended is common in this situation. This indicates that your astral self is ready to be liberated from its bodily confinement.

An emotional manifestation that precedes your astral projection can include a weight shifting feeling. Your body may suddenly feel heavy or very thin, as if its mass suddenly dropped or risen.

The natural temperature fluctuation can also be detected. The sensation of coldness, or the opposite, can be felt over you.

Vibrations or your spiritual frequency are the mental energy that all living things have. They are a spectrum of good and bad vibrations. Higher vibrations indicate more positive energies.

When we talk about keeping a high vibrancy or developing high waves, it means cultivating these higher energies. You can do it in many different ways.

1. Get rid of all toxic substances, such as alcohol and cigarettes, tobacco, pesticides, narcotics, and pollution from the environment. Eat healthy, breathe fresh air, and buy organic food. Exercise is a great way to detox. This is a great method

to detox. Apart from detoxing your body, this is also a great way for your mind to cleanse.

2. Be aware of the people in your social circle. Your energy and vibrations can be influenced greatly by the people you surround yourself with. Be sure to surround yourself with people who are calm, reliable, honest, and positive. They will also boost your energy. If you find this daunting, think about the six people who are closest to you. They have the greatest influence.

3. You can practice compassion with others and yourself. Kindness has a way to lift our vibrations. Being compassionate can be as simple as praying for others or volunteering. You can also be kind by giving of your time or volunteering. It is also about being kind to yourself. That means you should forgive yourself and be open to forgiveness. See the oneness and

commonalities between yourself and others. You should also be grateful for what is available to you and offer your help to someone less fortunate.

4. Meditate. Meditation is a well-studied and long-standing practice. It is being studied today and has been shown to be extremely beneficial for the mind. There are thousands upon thousands of meditation methods. While some meditation experts will tell you that it is important to sit in a certain place, chant, or think particular thoughts in order to deepen your meditation, there are thousands of ways to do so. If it is hard to sit on a post, you can use a chair or lay down. This will align your spine as well as your chakras. If you are unable to think of loving thoughts, images, and mantras, then try focusing on one thing. You could also visual practice meditation or just calm your mind. Meditation can increase your

vibrations because you are more connected to yourself and with the energies flowing throughout the universe.

5. You can also journal every day, weekly or as often as you like. Journaling can be a powerful tool for self-discovery. Journaling allows you to feel connected to yourself, see changes in your life, and can help you understand your inner world. You may even be able to see messages from higher self through the journal entries. This will surely increase your vibrations.

Simply put, any action you take or word that brings joy, joy, love and goodness into your heart and soul will elevate your vibrations. Concentrate on the fact that there are order and wholeness in the universe.

Now that you know how to raise vibrations to a high level, let's learn more about how to achieve the right mindset for astral projection. Although there are many different methods for astral projection, there are the most basic guidelines that will help you get there.

You can find some helpful guidelines to help you prepare for an exhilarating experience.

1. Start in morning. Get up when you are most awake. This will make you feel more relaxed. Your awareness won't kick in because of the drowsiness you still feel. Even if you don't get up in the morning to do astral projection, you can still do it at any hour. You just need to find what you like and be able to execute it.

2. The right atmosphere is important. To ensure you feel at ease, you should do it in your home.

If you don't want to project astral images with others, it is better to do it alone. To avoid distractions from others walking around your home or walking in on you, do it in a different place or in a completely separate room.

Make sure you draw the shades, so you don't get distracted by the outside world. Any kind of interruption or noise can disrupt your state of relaxation.

3. Focus on positive thoughts. Astral projection may be hindered if you are too stressed out by everyday life. A positive mindset is more likely for positive astral experiences.

4. Relax, and lay down. Once you have chosen your bedroom, you can then relax by laying down on your back. Clear your mind and distract from distractions. It is important to pay attention to your body and how it feels.

Start with your feet and work your way up to your head. Relax your legs and work your way up towards your head. This will allow you to relax all your muscles.

Do not tension your chest and shoulders. Relax and take long, deep breaths. Be sure to exhale fully after you take your next breath.

You can keep your mind from drifting to outside thoughts by focusing on your breath.

According to some, holding a quartz crystal can increase and speedup the vibrations of your body. If you decide to do this, be sure to place the crystal on the third eye chakra. This is just above the center of the eyebrows.

Feel the vibrations of the crystal moving through your body after you have placed it on your head. You may find it useful to visualise a certain color.

After you are able to astral project, you can place the crystal on your chest or in your hands. The glass has two purposes: it protects you from negative energy and empowers you.

To avoid getting distracted by tension in the muscles, relax your whole body. It will be harder to manifest your astral projections if you have anxiety or other distractions.

You can relax by going into meditation if necessary before you attempt to project your astral body.

Chapter 9: How to get out of the body

Astral Projection Techniques

Diverse cultures found their own ways to access the astral realms. This is great news for those who are open to trying different methods until they find the one that works best.

While it is not impossible, astral projection does not come easily to everyone. Many of us grew up in a world that focuses on physical evidence and spiritual reality, making it difficult to make changes. It can be hard to get rid of our cultural conditioning. This can make it difficult for us to reach the astral realms. You will need to practice getting past these mental anchors. Be positive and continue practicing your chosen techniques until you achieve success.

Blue Wave Technique

Blue wave technique may be the most popular and efficient method of inducing telepathic projection. Guided meditation can be used to initiate astral projections. It allows you to take control of the process and is very effective.

Blue wave techniques have a drawback. This level of control makes letting go of fear, conditioning, and conditioning difficult. People who wish to experience astral projection in a more gradual manner, instead of jumping headfirst into other techniques, can practice guided meditation. When selecting your astral projection method, it is crucial to understand your limitations and abilities.

Ear Nose Technique

The Ear nose Method is probably the most popular. Robert Bruce is credited for developing the Ear nose Technique

Meditation and deep breathing are two ways to get yourself into a trance. Relaxation is key to not falling asleep. You can focus on a specific object in the space and gaze at it until you are able to see it clearly in your mind's eyes. If you're ready to increase your relaxation, close the eyes and keep the object's image inside your mind. This will help keep your brain alert when your body starts to fall asleep.

You will start to feel a weird vibrating sensation within your body. This is your energy body. Allow yourself to feel the excitement.

Before you can pull out of your body, it is important to master how vibrations work. You can't control what happens to your body without having that level of control. Use your willpower to control the frequency and times they occur. Once you've achieved complete control over the vibrations you can move onto the next step.

Next, imagine a rope hanging from your ceiling and hanging over you. Visualize your energy hands rising from your physical hands to grab this rope. "Sensitize" to the line, its texture, width, and other details. Stop when you feel confident in the firmness and stability of your vision. Bring yourself back into your alert state.

You can control the experience even more by taking a short break between a partial and full separation. Continue the steps above until you reach the rope. But this time, you'll keep going. Slowly start to pull down on that line. As you do this, your energetic body will move up and away from your body. This will cause the vibration to increase in frequency, and intensity. You might feel your body paralyzed or even paralyzed while doing this. Continue on until you are completely free of your physical body. Once you do, your astral body will become fully free.

You should only try your first time. Take a tour of your room from your astral body. Explore the walls. Then, explore the other rooms in your house.

Detachment Technique

Robert Monroe is a recognized expert in astral travel and developed this technique.

First, you need to induce a hypnagogic mental state to be able practice the Detachment Technik. This is a mental state that allows us to be alert while we are between sleeping and rising. Meditation and relaxation are the first steps to achieve deep relaxation without falling asleep.

You are now completely relaxed and have entered hypnagogic mode. Relax even further to deepen your state. You can maintain your alertness by gazing at the dark behind your eyes. Next, inducing the vibrational state described under the Rope Technique is necessary. Following a similar pattern as the vibrations start, relax into them then learn to control. As the waves grow stronger, your energetic body is ready and able to leave your physical and mental body. Mentally roll your body over so that you can get out on your bed. From there you can move freely as you please.

Display Technique

While this simple technique is not difficult to master, it can be very useful for those who are visually-oriented. You can achieve a trance-like state by following the steps in the exercises. The visualization section of the exercise can be started when you're in a deep, relaxing state.

Begin to pay attention to your feet. Try to see your energetic feet among the physical ones. Slowly extend the active feet of your foot just a bit beyond your physical one. After a while, bring your energetic foot back into the physical. Next, pay attention to your head. You will again see your lively head inside your physical body. Now, extend your energetic ear about an inch beyond the physical boundary of your head. Then hold for a while, then bring your head back in.

Get back down to the feet. Move your energetic feet approximately two inches further than your physical feet and then bring them in. You can do the same thing with your head. Repeat this motion with your head, moving back and forth between them until you reach two feet beyond the limit of your physical body. Continue to rock until you reach the vibrational state. Once you have controlled the vibrations and are ready to move, stretch your mind.

After you have learned the preparation techniques, and you have reached the vibrational condition, you are ready for separation from your physical body. You can still reach the vibrational states but you cannot separate from your body.

At this stage, the biggest obstacle is to accurately respond to what's happening. Most people know a lot about astral projection and have expectations about what it will feel like. To ensure they are on track, they keep an eye out for certain milestones.

But, you should keep your eyes on your physical body. Once you've reached vibrational status, the best thing is to shift your focus away from your physical body.

To make sure you're moving in the right direction you must keep your eyes on every sensation in your body. This will help you to stay focused and it will likely prove difficult to separate. Instead of paying attention and focusing on all the feelings you have, try to focus your attention away from yourself.

It is likely that you will have difficulty shifting your focus away from any physical sensations the first few attempts you make to separate. It is normal. You will need to go through this process several times before you are able to forget the emotions and move on.

To focus your attention on something else, you can use a variety of separation techniques. You need to find the one that suits you best.

Now I'll be discussing several different detachment methods. After you have mastered these techniques, you will be able to select the one that is right for you.

Countdown Technique

The vibrational state is when your astral bodies separate from your body. You may be able to just float, stand up, or roll off your body at this point. It is enough to give yourself an encouragement to get outside.

Just focus on floating upward and moving away from your body. Imagine yourself floating around like a balloon. A balloon could lift you up as it floats through the air.

To get out of your body, your spirit body will stand up and walk out from your body. It will feel very much like you are sitting up in a physical body. Simply sit up normally and don't think about it.

To roll out, visualize your astral self doing a sideways roll of your physical body.

While all these techniques are similar, the movements of each one are slightly different. You may find one works better than the other, so make sure to try all of them.

Rotation Technique

Another way is to think of moving to project your astral bodies out. There are many ways to imagine what you can do with your body.

One way to visualize yourself leaping out of your own body is by using the "Imagine" technique. As your astral body bounces higher and higher on a trampoline you can imagine it separating from your physical body.

You can also imagine your astral self as a rocket propelling itself out of you body. Your astral body can be visualized being pulled back like an arrow, and then flying out of your body.

It is possible to imagine your astral self swinging higher and higher. Your astral body could also be seen swinging as high and getting out of your body.

Another way is to picture your astral body moving or rocking side-to-side like you're in a hammock. Imagine your astral being able to move backwards and forwards until it is free from your physical body.

Chapter 10: Returning to Your Bodily Health

As magical as an astral journey can be, there will always come a time when one must return to the world of physical reality and take care of loved ones.

Knowing When to Return

The astral realm doesn't have time, so it's easy for people to lose sight of time while they explore the cosmos. It's not usually a problem if your travels are over, but it might be an issue for your body to be neglected for hours at time. Keep in mind the importance of maintaining a healthy body by nourishing it and keeping it hydrated.

Although it can be very relaxing to get away from the physical world and see the universe as it is, it is best not to spend too much time in the astral realm unless you have a spiritual occupation. You can lose control of physical reality if you spend too much time in the astral realm. If you dream of going back to the Astral realm, it will make it hard to concentrate on your job.

It is true that all spiritual beings can experience the physical realm as human beings; this is what it means. There are some reasons that we came here. These include experiencing the material. It is important to remember that you will spend most of the time here, not where you originally planned to.

The Return Journey

Astral travel can make it very easy to return. Think about your physical body to instantly travel there. Some people can instantly fall back into it when they see their bodies. Others will need to lie down to get back in.

Others may need a gradual return to health. The abruptness of snapping in and out can be disruptive. Shamanic practitioners mostly use a method to transition back, before returning to their bodies. If you want to go back in time, you can retrace your steps. You can set your alarm to send you a single alert to let your body know that it is time to begin transitioning back. When it is, the last alarm will sound to remind you to go to your body and get back to your awareness.

Grounding

It is essential to stay grounded once you have returned. To become physically active again, you can move your fingers and arms. If you feel paralysed from sleep, try shaking your head until you regain control.

Grounding meditation is when you are awake and alert. This meditation can be done standing, sitting, or standing. As you visualize roots growing from the ground of your feet and reaching into the Earth, picture them. You can then plunge them down into the centre and begin to draw energy from the Earth's center into your roots. Begin at your feet and fill yourself up with earth energy until you are grounded. Continue doing this until you feel comfortable.

After Care

Remember to eat as soon as your body is ready to drink. For further grounding, nuts and fruits can be a great way to get in touch with earth energy. Take some meat if you have trouble feeling grounded or shaking off the floaty, woozy feeling.

Allow yourself to sleep as much or as little as you need after returning from your trips. Your body needs to have the chance to reset and balance itself. It takes some time to get used to psychic work. So be gentle with your body, take good care and stay well.

What can I do to make it come back?

All good things must come an end. Unfortunately, that includes astral projections. In order to live a healthy life, you will need to return to this world. An overwhelming sense of peace, love, or raised consciousness should guide you back to that feeling. You might also feel tired and overwhelmed. All of these emotions are perfectly normal and understandable. Only you have ever lived through it. Some people can find it overwhelming. You have done something extraordinary.

The umbilical cord connects the astral with the material and allows you to return to your body. It will lead you home, allowing your astral body and soul to be reconnected. As with all aspects of astral projecting, this purposeful linking will be positive and uplifting.

You'll follow the silver chord to your destination, just like they did in the Wizard of Oz. It is simple as that. You will find your silver cord wherever you go in the astral realm. It will also be there as a liaison between your physical body in the spiritual realm and your astral body.

You can now return to your physical self and stop astral projection. All you need to do is grab your silver cord to take you home. If you want it to happen immediately, it will. Concepts such as time, distance, etc. They have no meaning and are not relevant to the spiritual realm. You decide how to get there, as with all of your travels. You can simply snap your fingers to get back into your physical body. You may want to visualize yourself following the silver rope as a guide or following a path made of breadcrumbs. You have the option to fly, canoe, or use a cannon. However you feel most comfortable, that is the best way for your return trip. Let your imagination guide you and let it unfold.

To remind you when your astral projector session is over, it's a good idea to set up a timer. It's easy to lose sight of time when you get more involved in this practice. Particularly since matter, time, and space are all irrelevant in the spiritual realm. Although it can appear that time outside of your body may be minutes, it can also seem to be hours. It is crucial to not spend all of the time astral projecting. You need to get enough sleep, rest and exercise, as well as time to live your normal life: eating, sleeping, working, playing and exercising. You can use a gentle timer to signal that it is time you grab the silver cable and start following it home. It is also ok to turn the timer off when it wakes you. Use the remaining minutes to complete any project, conversation, or other journey you are having, then you can follow the silver cable home to your physical self. It shouldn't sound too loud, like an alarm. But, it should be soothing and rhythmic, such as chanting or rhythmic gongs.

You will most likely regain consciousness after you have returned to your body. Technically, it is not like you are waking up. However, that is the easiest description of the feeling of returning. It is different than leaving, which takes more effort. You are more honest and faster when you return. Instantly, you are right back where you started.

It is crucial to conduct a system review on yourself to determine how you feel. It's likely that you'll feel both invigorated, and slightly dazed, at first. You're now motivated because you have just accomplished something extraordinary and exceptional. The same reasons could cause you to be stunned. It can be overwhelming for some people. You might also feel stiffened or unused depending on how much time you've been projecting. Spend a few minutes getting to know your body again and re-acquaint yourself with the physical world. Allow yourself to feel the feelings that you have received from the astral plane. Keep the sensations that you feel heightened consciousness, love, and peaceful. For many people, this is the reason why they started astral projection.

You can spend a few minutes here to help you return to the physical realm. Remain relaxed and concentrate on your breathing. The positive feelings you bring back will have an impact on your daily life. An example of a good mantra would be "I'll remember", which can help your brain retain the information. When you repeat the phrase, pay close attention.

These ideas will help you transfer your knowledge from there into your physical mind. Astral projection is a way to increase your awareness and build on your existing knowledge. It is similar to making a New year's resolution. You will likely remember these lessons more often than you think, especially because you can astralproject as many times per year as you wish.

You will notice a significant increase in your spiritual growth through the transfer of energy between the astral and this realm. There are no limits, so your consciousness will grow exponentially through your journeys. This is exciting and transformative. It should be something you enjoy. These benefits will show up in all aspects of your life, such as in your personal relationships, at work and in your overall happiness and enjoyment. Astral projection allows you to see endless possibilities. Your imagination doesn't have to be limited. Without these limitations, you can definitely make a big difference.

Chapter 11: Returned difficulties

Headaches and pressure around the forehead

While activating the third eye, feel pressure can be common on the forehead. It is caused by focusing too much attention on one area and trying to redirect your energy towards it. It will go away quickly if you have such headaches. But for some people, the tension can last several hours even after they have finished with their meditation. It's okay to feel this way if it happens to you. This is normal during the initial stages. It is a sign your third eye is being stimulated.

Tingling sensation

Also, you may feel a tingling sensation in your forehead as well as other areas of the body. This sensation can last up to a few days or hours after the process is completed. But, it is only temporary, and you should not be alarmed.

Migraines

Migraine headaches can cause severe pain. They can be very painful. These headaches usually last for a few more days. Your physician should be consulted if you think the problem you are having is related to meditation. You can make the problem worse by not paying enough attention.

Seeing Strange Shapes

Many people see odd shapes very soon after their third-eye activation meditation. If you're in this category, it is not a reason to panic. Meditation involves looking for light while focusing for long periods. This can sometimes lead to images in your brain. Most often, it's an image of light shapes or an eye.

Vivid Dreams and Nightmares

People can have lucid fantasies or dreams. Your mental vision can become more vivid when you activate your 3rd eye. It could lead to such fantasies. It does not pose any other danger but it can cause insomnia and restlessness in some people. You can calm your mind if this is the case. Such dreams occur when your thoughts become too wild. Meditation is the only remedy for these thoughts. Calm your mind and focus on positive thoughts. These ideas can be caused by excessive accumulations of negative thoughts.

Third eye activation allows you to control your mind and avoid being controlled. It will enable you to use the power of your mind as you wish. Third eye awakening isn't for everyone. If you are afflicted by addictions or a weak heart, third eye activation should be avoided.

How much fear are you able to bear?

Fear of the unknown is part of your personality

Fear is a natural phenomenon. Everyone has a fear. Ghosts, spirits, ghosts and other paranormal entities can cause fear in anyone. It can be helpful if you have a healthy fear about such entities. You should not activate your third eye until you feel comfortable with your fears. If you are not careful, your paranoia will increase and you will feel restless.

Schizophrenia has already struck.

Schizophrenia, a severe mental disorder, is where you switch between reality and illusions. With such a condition, practicing third eye meditation can be dangerous. This will make it more complicated. Schizophrenia is a condition that can cause strange symptoms. Such people are strongly advised not to enter this dimension.

You have succumbed the drug addiction: psychosis and constant hallucination

If you're practicing third eye awakening, any kind of addiction is wrong. Addictions can make your mental health worse and cause you to lose your ability to focus. The dangers of using drugs and other addictive behaviors can be severe. You could get worse results if you mix third eye meditation with drug use. For some, psychosis and permanent hallucination may become a reality. It can be difficult to treat these conditions and you might never get out of it. Mixing addictions with third eye awakening should be avoided.

The third eye should be used to establish a connection between spirits and you.

Some people believe they can use the powers and abilities of the third-eye to communicate with the senses. This is a possibility but you should not do it. It is impossible to comprehend the full range of senses and energies. This energy system includes only a small portion of us. Being a part of energies outside your control spectrum can prove dangerous. Their power cannot be measured. You should only use the third-eye awakening to bring about good and beneficial things. If you are able to communicate with ghosts or spirits, you could attract strong negative energies.

You haven't researched well

You should not enter into any relationship without first researching it thoroughly. Third eye activation is something you should research carefully. Do your research to learn more about the process. It should meet your goals. Only then should this realm be entered. A futile quest will cost you a lot of energy and time.

Fear of astral projection and the Biggest Mistakes

If you don't do something, it is doing it wrong. Third eye activation can be the same. If you do not know how to activate your third-eye, you could end up with some really bad results. Third eye awakening requires a lot of dedication and care.

You will not find instant gratification or quick results if you're looking for immediate results. Some people give up trying, but they never succeed with activating their third eyes. They may not be missing their third eye; rather, they are looking for it incorrectly. Failing to understand the signs and misinterpreting them can result in failure or despair.

These are some of the common mistakes people make when activating their third-eye. You should avoid them.

You indulge in misinformation

Misinformation can easily be spread via TV, media, or the internet. They have the ability to make a mountain out a molehill. They can convince you of ridiculous things which may cause desperation at the end. It is important to be aware of the challenges you may face on your path to activating your third eye. It is important to recognize the gaps and avoid getting lost. Do your research before you start the journey of activating third eye.

Trust is lacking

Trust is crucial when embarking on any adventure. Third eye activation offers an adventure trip unlike any others. It requires trust in your own abilities and intuitions to enjoy it. You should trust what you feel and see while activating your 3rd eye. Also, you must give importance to any changes you encounter along the way. It is essential to remain aware of all the little things.

Manufacture without a Purpose

People without a clear reason for activating their 3rd eye will have problems. It's not an easy task to enable the third eyes. You cannot get it out of your system as easily as you can with other things. It causes irreversible damage. To activate the third eye, you must have a purpose. Only then will it be possible to gauge the extent of your success in your pursuits. You might not find the right thing if you aren't looking for it.

Technique is lacking

To activate the third eye, it is essential to use a good technique. It can seem like there is no clear path for activating your third eye. While the path to inner peace doesn't follow a specific route, using the right techniques can help you avoid feeling lost. Select the best method for you and be sure to follow it. If you don't change your methods, you could lose all your progress. Be consistent with your practice and give it your all. People who do this lightly will end up wasting their time.

You try too hard

Don't push yourself too hard. People who want to achieve quick success often start by trying too hard at first. You may end up desperation or your mind will make up false stories. Both can lead you to failure. Focus on the technique to activate your third-eye and let it happen. Try not to force your mind into thinking a certain way. An excessive dependence on visualization can lead to false ideas being formed in your mind. You might find yourself seeing things you like, without actually having accomplished anything.

Don't Look for the Wrong Signs

Look for the right signs. Some people who claim to be experts in third eye activation have made some incorrect assumptions. They believe that third eye activation only happens if someone gets certain signs. This is false. Pay attention to the subtle changes that are taking place within you. Trust your gut and take control. Do not believe in false notions. Different experiences with third eye awakening might be possible. It is possible to never be satisfied if your eyes keep on the experiences of others.

No Instant Results

Third eye activation can be compared to placing an order on the internet. It may not occur immediately. It might take some time before your third eye is able to detect a change. Learning to be a better person takes time and practice. This aspect should be taken very seriously.

You don't have enough practice

This is a continuation to the previous point. For you to achieve measurable results, your skills will need to be practiced for some time. It doesn't matter if your third eyes are active. If you do not practice it often, it won't give you any significant results. You must train your brain to look in the right directions. Your brain must learn to recognize signs. It should be able to look at the world with better understanding. Meditation should be an integral part of your daily schedule. Do not make excuses, miss it or ignore it. Doing so will only lead to failure.

Avoid Overpublicizing Your Efforts

It takes a lot of effort to awaken your third vision. It is a long process and not all are easy. You should not talk about it to anyone. Negative criticisms and envy can result from such discussions. You might find yourself being ridiculed or labeled. This could lead to doubts. Keep it to your self and practice.

Chapter 12: The Hypothesis of How to Exit With Illusory Movement

Many possible explanations, though purely theoretical for this phenomenon, exist. As I projected myself into the astral world, I was aware that I regained consciousness within this body. Keep in mind that knowledge is lost to the astral body at the beginning of the period

"Unconsciousness." The physical body does not cause the loss of consciousness. The astral body can exist outside of the physical and be conscious or unconscious. It is also possible to be unconscious in the body. Although they are two distinct phenomena, the astral body exit and the loss in knowledge are often co-occurring. If the astral bodies leave the physical and we lose consciousness, then the conscious astral projection will not exist. The body that is in a trance before falling asleep already enters the resting zone. This allows the astral to retain consciousness and then experience repercussion. This happens quite often. The astral body only enters the rest area for a brief moment before the knowledge is switched off. This led many occultists and others to believe that astral bodies exit causes consciousness loss. But this is an error.

It is also true, that the astral body can remain unconscious for some time in the physical world before it enters the rest area. This applies in situations where a stimulant affects the body. These are exceptions. The astral body is usually able to leave the physical world immediately after turning off consciousness. This may happen in a short time for some people or it can take longer depending on your condition. It is simple to see that conscious projection is possible only if the transition from the rest zone is preceded by the shutdown. As we have seen, several factors contribute to this condition: temperament, physical pasivity, and other.

If consciousness eventually leaves us, when the astral bodies are unconscious, then knowledge must be removed from the collection. When the astral bodies still have part of consciousness, then the knowledge must be half taken. If the subject is able to see the astral body's movements and then enters into it, it may be that the portion of consciousness taken from his body was able to function in this manner. You may also dream that another subtle body was watching the astral and separated from it.

Mental stimulation is the best way to generate the stress necessary for projection. How about creating a habit that doesn't have to do with screening? This will cause the subconscious mind to feel "stressed" and you can then cultivate a desire to project yourself. As a result, you will see dreams that are fully compatible with real life and not through habit.

Meditation Should Be Praised

You should meditate every day, for a fast and efficient technique. Respect the rules and follow them.

It is essential to harness the power inherent in each of these chakras so that you can balance your strengths. When you have all the electricity necessary to balance the various chakras, it's easy to project in an astral manner.

Chapter 13: False Awakening

This is often interpreted as a Lucid Dream, but it is actually not true Lucid Dreaming. In this type, the dreamer "awakes" to find themselves in a different or the exact same room as they expect (the bed they slept in). The individual may begin their morning routine but then wake up to find that they have been interrupted. This could be false awakenings or real things. Only then does consciousness kick in, and the individual will realise that they are dreaming. Each person has an astral body that is an absolute double of their physical body. It is made of subtle, etheric matter and is typically enclosed in a human body. Separating the astral from the physical body is difficult in ordinary circumstances. However, in certain cases, such as dreams or extreme mental stress or under conditions of occult developmental, the astral bodies can be released and sent on a long journey that travels at a slower rate than light waves. The astral body is linked with the physical through a long thin thread. In practice, it is extremely rare for this to happen. Although it remains in existence for a long period of time after death of the physical body's owner, the astral bodies eventually begin to decay. Sometimes, it is mistaken for a spirit of the deceased and hovers near the burial place. It is simply a thin shell of the soul or a shell. In the moments prior to physical death, the astral body often appears in the company of close friends and family. This phenomenon is caused by the deceased's strong desire for visibility and sight. The astral bodies often leave their physical counterparts during psychopathic phenomena, and visit distant places to feel that something is taking place. It may also leave the body under the influence or deeper stages of hypnosis during psychosomatic dreams. It will then visit unfamiliar places and scenes and engage in conversation with other astral body or less human beings. Because the brain did not receive clear impressions from inadequate training, development and so forth, it creates mixed or distorted memories that look like a darkened, damaged photographic plate. The possibility that the reader already believes in the existence of the phenomenon or is interested enough to accept the fact, I am willing to admit. We won't discuss spiritualism as a whole, since it doesn't help with the problem. This is because there are other books that deal with the subject by far more knowledgeable authors than me. We focus on the unusual behavior of the astral bodily during life. Although, as I mentioned, it also exists after death. Other works speak about its future. Our interest lies in studying the astral bodies before their physical double is forever separated. Our material part, while physically alive, is more dead than a doornail. This is the energy which exists behind the physical mechanisms, and it is truly "living". Nerves do not exist. In fact, if they were alive we would have buried far too many people. Their nervous energy is what makes them live, and your astral body acts as a capacitor for the nervous energy you're currently using.

Prompting Lucid Dreams

There are three ways that we can reach the Lucid Dream. These are.

* Dream Initiation and Lucid Dreams (DILD).

* Mnemonic initiation of Lucid Nights (MILD).

* Waking initiation for Lucid Dreams

DILD

This is the most natural and common way Lucid Dreams happen. The dreamer falls asleep and begins to dream. The dreamer's conscious brain, or portions thereof, becomes more reactive during the dream. Consequently, they become aware that they are actually dreaming. These dreams often reflect their mundane nature. The idea's events will either be every day or not at all unusual. One aspect of the goal might seem unusual or the experience may not be familiar. The dreamer begins to realize that they are dreaming and starts to feel control over the dream. This is the type of Lucid Dream that most people will experience. But there is no way to know how. You will probably experience it at some point in your lifetime, but this is the easiest form of Lucid Dreaming.

MILD

Stephen LaBerge, an expert in Lucid Dreaming, pioneered this technique. The method works by training your mind to recognize that you dream. It's actually very easy. This is a simple technique that involves creating a habit during sleep, and then continuing to do so while you are asleep. You should recognize the activity as a sign that your dreaming is occurring. This sounds complicated, but it is really quite easy. Some suggestions include counting your fingers while awake, ideally before you go to bed. You can look at each one and try to visualize them in your head. After counting and staring at them for a while you can relax and fall asleep. After falling asleep, the brain can begin its task of organizing and analysing the day's events. It might not deal with the final thing first. However, it is possible to achieve some success by using this technique. You must consider your visual perception. The fingers may seem to be more many than they need to be or might be missing in your dream. This is your cue that you're dreaming. The moment you wake up, the conscious mind is reactivated. From this point on, you can control your dream. The MILD technique is very useful for beginners. You can activate it in days or even weeks.

WILD

This technique can be more difficult than MILD and requires more practice. In DILD and MILD techniques to initiate Lucid Dreaming, an individual falls asleep and experiences dreams. After the dream, part of their consciousness is switched back on. You want to keep your conscious "switched up" during sleep so you can fall asleep in a dream state. You can achieve this by using relaxation techniques and meditation. Your goal is to just fall asleep while your awareness remains partly focused. This technique can be very useful at certain times during the sleep cycle. If REM goes off-line, it will be reactivated when you go to sleep. To induce dreaming, get up earlier than usual or take a quick nap. You can use this combination with a relaxation strategy to help you fall asleep quickly to have a Lucid Dream.

Note: This technique is most likely to cause sleep paralysis, which can occur when you fall asleep. You might experience loss of motion, a feeling of falling, or strange visions and sounds. This is perfectly normal. It happens every time we go to sleep. But, in normal circumstances, we don't notice it. You should be ready for a few strange experiences if you try this method.

Chapter 14: Successes, Failures: The Key to Reading

It is known that healthy sleep results in the body being more or less passive. To make this condition even more severe, it is essential to slow down the heartbeat. This truth is what I discovered, as I've already explained to you. It was also possible to slow the pulse. Exercise can slow the pulse. It contributes to concentration and relaxation. When you are ready to go to bed, your first task is to find a comfortable horizontal position. If you have trouble with your back, try lying on your right side. However, you should be lying on the back, with your arms stretched out on your hands. First, take a deep breath. Take a moment to hold your breath. Next, direct your breathing to the upper abdomen so that the diaphragm raises. Repeat this six to eight times. This will relax the solar plexus. Dr Carrington's book about yoga offers some useful advice. He advises that you feel the relaxation of solar plexus and to consciously see it expand like a flower slightly below the spot where the spines diverge. Focus on the solarplexus to feel this. Once you do, you can relax. The solarplexus is similar to an octopus. The solar plexus and the heart will be put under pressure if this happens.

Next, close the eyes and picture yourself. Think about your scalp starting at the top. Then, move towards the back, straining the muscles. Next, consider the neck. You can tighten it a few times and then relax its muscles. You can then rest your hand on the top of your fingers. Next, raise your hands and relax your fingers. Beginning at the neck base, begin to go down. Once you reach the bottom, stretch and relax your muscles. Is she a cat?

Now, pay attention to the heart. Soon, you will start to feel his beat in the same part of the chest. Keep your attention on his knocks until it becomes clear.

These ripples can be felt in the backside of the head during projection. These are the only physical sensations that you feel, if the blanket is not in your hands. It is easiest for a person to hear a heartbeat while lying on their back. This is not desirable. After learning to lie still and to hear and feel your pulse (you will most likely gain this ability in just a few short experiments), you can then learn to listen to and feel pulsations from all parts of your body. Let's say you have now positioned yourself according to my instructions. Now listen (feel) for a heartbeat. It is important to pay attention.

Now focus your attention on your neck. Do you feel your heartbeat beating in your throat or chest? If so, reach for the cheeks. These are where you will hear distinct knocks. Focus on the top of you head. You will feel a ripple in you head. Now, focus on your top. Now you feel a pulse in the upper stomach. Don't move to the next body part until you are comfortable with them. Now, concentrate on your lower abdomen. These pulsations are almost as clear as those heard on the neck. Moving slowly towards the hips, then the calves and finally the feet. Now return to the calves. Do you feel any changes in the calves? Focus on your hips and keep them there. You can now see them. Now, place your focus on your right thigh. You should feel the heartbeat in every part of your body. If your feet freeze again, you can warm them up the same way.

The sensation of pulsation occurring in the area of the Medulla Oblongata is completely similar to that of a ghost (through astral cord).

Be aware that a sick heart should not be projected onto the astral body. It is your life factor and depends on breathing. It is extremely dangerous to damage a already weak heart. There is nothing to be concerned about if your heart isn't too troubled.

Next is to slow the ripple down, which is very easy. Astral projection requires a steady and slow heartbeat. Focus on this organ and imagine you are one mind and your heart is the other, with the former being able understand and obey the language of both. Your thoughts, or concentration, is independent. You can slow down or speed up the heartbeat by imagining that this mind controls it. You may have tried to send your thoughts or orders directly to the subconscious, but then you asked yourself "How do i know if my suggestions convince the subconscious?" This is how you know your heart. Many people are disappointed by their ability to make suggestions after the first attempt. They won't repeat the idea until it is ingrained in their subconscious. But wait! What if our subconscious minds followed the first thoughts we had? Imagine your heart stopping and your inner mind immediately following this decision. The subconscious mind is difficult to control but it is easy to speed up or slow down the heartbeat.

Let's start from the beginning. You lay on your stomach, your arms extended over your body and feel the heartbeat. Again, you are focusing on your heart. If it doesn't beat evenly, suggest something else. Continue this process until your heart beats consistently. Now just focus on the pulsation in your heart. Pay attention to the beats, and count them mentally. After a few minutes, you can begin to count the beats a bit slower. Imagine that your soul is already beating faster.

Continue to probe the heart to see if it is responding to your suggestion. Keep at it until your heart starts beating at the desired pace. It's impossible to know exactly how slow your heart should beat to ensure you are physically passive. My heart rate for regular projections was 42 beats/minute. A pulse of this magnitude is not dangerous. However, it indicates a great deal of passivity. It is known that the pulse slows during sleep. My daily pulse would be 42 beats. Then it would slow down significantly at night. The average heart rate of different people will vary. It is your responsibility to determine your level of passivity. If the room becomes cold before you fall asleep or if you feel that you can take a deep breath and it feels like you are breathing in fresh air, then you have attained the right degree of passivity. It is important to not feel uncomfortable. It is important to create a comfortable environment that allows you to be cool but also comfortable.

You can also experiment with normal levels of passiveness during sleep if your heart rate is too fast. However, it is important to remember that the chances of success are greater if your body is less active. The physical condition of the body determines the location of the rest zones. A ghost is defined as extreme passiveness and fatigue. The ghost can leave the physical body by walking 2 feet. You may find that you do not fall asleep if you're not exhausted and have plenty of energy. When you do fall asleep, the astral body is separated from the physical by only a fraction. The ghost can be separated up to 6 inches depending on the combination of factors. A dream that is deeper and more vivid causes a spirit to rise higher. Most projections happen after several hours of sleeping.

The heart will respond with surprising ease when you slow down its pulse. So, for example, you could say: "Heart. Now you must make 50 beats a minute, and continue doing this until you receive more instructions." Don't check your heart for hours. It can weaken suggestion. You need to trust your heart if it is your goal to control it. My understanding is that controlling your heart is the only way you can achieve physical passivity. This is the key to astral projection. You can also practice it by becoming more self-aware. You must ensure that all elements are in place to allow you to manifest yourself.

The unique thing about this phenomenon is its inability to move. Because it isn't yet known, I called it "astral calamity". You will find that astral-catalepsy can be accompanied or triggered by feelings.

The sticking sensation was gone, and replaced by an entirely different feeling:

soaring. The simultaneous sensation caused my completely numb physical body to vibrate at a high speed, up and downward, even though I assumed it was a body. I felt tremendous pressure at my back in the vicinity of the Medulla Oblongata. The pressure was noticeable and manifested as jerks. My whole body began to pulsate from the force of these jerks. This seemed like a nightmare in absolute dark, as I did not understand what was happening. I learned to distinguish between familiar and far-off sounds amid the madness of bizarre sensations such as vibration, angular movements and soaring. The rumor was true. I tried to move, but I couldn't. It was almost as if a super-powerful and mysterious guiding force held me. When the hearing returned the vision began acting. I was surprised to see. It is impossible to express my amazement with words.

Chapter 15: Self awareness: The development of awareness

To improve self-awareness and confidence, use these tricks and tips to make it easier to do what you want. Astral projection isn't for everyone.

You can now follow these tips to help you achieve astral travel.

1. Look after your health! You are what is in your body. Consuming a raw or vegan diet will raise your vibration and improve the quality of your life. This will increase your success rate in the future.

2. Be calm. You must remain comfortable while you work towards astral projection. Practice relaxation techniques and breathing techniques before you try to pull your soul from the body.

3. Use sounds. Binaural beats can help you relax. These sounds will alter your brainwave frequency, which can help you

be more comfortable with astral projection.

4. Explore different approaches. There is no one method that will give you the best out of body experience. Find the best technique for you by trying different methods. For astral travel, you can use techniques like the Rope method or displaced consciousness technique.

5. Try out different times of the days. You don't have to travel at the same time as you do. To help you achieve your goal, it is a good idea to try falling into hypnosis at different times throughout the day. Some people may be more comfortable traveling when they wake up but are still not aware of the whole world. Others might find it easier to travel after having dealt with the stresses and worries of the day.

6. Be fearless Astral projection can seem scary. Fearing the sensations that your

body feels is perfectly normal. They are not to be feared, but should be welcomed. Fear can distract you from the things you love and make it harder to get back to the same state you achieved.

7. Be patient. Don't give up if you don't succeed at astral projection. It is possible to practice until you feel more confident.

8. Project. You must be able to communicate your desire to travel with your body and mind. You cannot travel simply because you are curious. You must have a strong desire to leave your body.

9. Learn more. Research has never caused any harm to anyone. In reality, the more knowledge you have, you'll be better off.

10. You must get away from your body. You can leave your body at any point. The tether linking your soul and your body can snap you back to it quickly, preventing you from being able to travel through this

astral realm. You can explore your surroundings, as well as any other locations around you.

11. Keep track of all your experiences. Keep a record of what happens when you have returned to the body. Keep a notebook and record all that you experienced, felt, smelled, and so on. You may be surprised by what you discover when you go exploring.

12. Meditate. This is an effective way to increase awareness. It will make it easier to lucid dream more often. Most importantly, your astral travels will become more comfortable if you increase awareness in the physical realm.

Dream Control

Many coincidences are determined in part by your state of mind at that moment. Once you have the ability to control the thoughts and feelings that come up, you will be able to make them happen. These dreams will allow your astral body to move forward rather than halt in the rest zones. In the future, it will be revealed that astral projections allow the subject to see, and upon waking up, see his body projected in an environment similar the one of a dream. You will be able to inducing desired thoughts through practice. Dream control is a technique for astral projection that can be done in a pleasant and effective manner. X. Carrington said the following: "There's a way to call up true dreams." It is essential to observe when the consciousness enters a state called rest while falling asleep.

Conducting such experiments on yourself will eventually lead to the development of the ability for you to consciously control your body until you fall asleep. It's fascinating to observe your thoughts and feelings during the immersion process.

You can do this by mentally creating a scene in front of your eyes and focusing your attention there. You can then consciously transfer your consciousness to the scene at the very end of a dream. After having trained yourself to a certain degree, you can transfer your consciousness directly into a state that is sleep. In this way you can achieve an incredible wholeness of your thoughts. There will be no gaps in the consciousness. You will be able to enter into the dream and see it consciously. This will be an authentic dream. You will then remember exactly what happened.

Is it possible for Mr. Carrington to know how precisely his instructions on "true" dreams correspond to the method of controlling dream that is used to bring an astral body into the physical worldto participate in a dream? You must bring the astral mind to the desired place, which subconsciously aligns with the consciousness-generated sleep. Once you have learned to promote positive or favoritonal projections, your astral bodies can enter a dream. This will allow you to either recall all the details when you wake up or go into a state where you dream. You will then be in a projected dream state.

Do You Know What It Really Is?

A lot of people need their experiences validated, especially in the first instance. Common questions when returning from an experience of astral projection is, "Was this experience real?"

Your own question can be answered by refining the meaning of reality to you. But, when answering the question, the most important thing is to ask yourself: What was the real effect of the experience? Is it something that brought you real healing?

Do you believe that if it had a real impact on you and your psyche, it doesn't really matter whether the experience was objectively "real"?

Please Share Your Experiences

Everyone longs to tell others about their travel experiences upon their return. This is similar to the desire to tell others about your vacation. It is okay to share your experiences and be supported by people who are open-minded.

Don't be discouraged if someone rejects your experience. Accepting a new reality in the spiritual world can dramatically change someone's view of the world. This isn't easy. Reacting negatively to your story is more about the person than it is about you. It is important to try to openly communicate with people who will be able to accept your story, even if it seems like they are only believing what you have said.

It is important to remember that not all spiritual experience are meant for sharing. Remember to keep a distance if something is sacred, or if you are told by a spiritual guide that you should not share the experience or message. It is impossible to know all the wisdom and it will only be a benefit for those who aren't experienced enough.

Overall, your return experience must be positive. Astral travel is a great way to learn and grow. You will find that your newfound wisdom will improve your everyday life, and bring happiness and joy to your days. It's possible to be open to the experience and you will see good results. The entire process was opposite to what I saw when I got out from bed. The ghost gradually fell while vibrating. It then suddenly fell, once again coincident with the physical body. Every muscle in my physical body twitched as pain, and it felt almost like I was being smashed from head to foot at the moment of connection. I was physically awake again, filled with awe and fear; I was aware of everything that was happening.

Since that experience, I have had many other projections. Some of these sensations were different from what I was describing, but all of them involved the same body movement route. Although repetition brings more perfection, it was probably the most extraordinary first projection I have ever experienced.

It was also clearer than any of the best attempts by experienced mediums. While I do believe in my inner projection skills, I attribute the first exteriorization's exclusiveness to the fact I was surrounded by other unusual mediums.

This is an important fact that many who practice occultism understand: one person can benefit from another by establishing a "line" of power.

Let's get on with it. The ability to interrupt consciousness can occur at any time and in any place. This phenomenon may be mixed with loss consciousness or complete ignorance. Consciousness is usually involved when the astral body separates and it moves.

It is completely unaware of this until the time that awakening occurs. This is the most desirable type of intervention. In this example, the undesirable and initial stages are removed from the consciousness of the subject. The unconsciously controlled steps of catalepsy, erratic moves, and soaring are the first.

These steps can be unpleasant for the included consciousness, but they can quickly become insensitive. These stages occur even though the subject is unconscious.

Chapter 16: Sex and Astral Projections: Physically Projection

The sexdrive is just like any other vital muscle or brain function. The more you use it, the better it gets. You stop using it. It gets flabby, out of form. How many times have you seen a "couch potatoes" with a great body? You probably haven't. This principle also applies to sex drives. If you stop sex due to other commitments or exhaustion, then your sex drive can become dead.

Your sex drive isn't always conscious. The following are reasons your sex drives start to slow down:

1. Depression and anxiety, as well as their medications.

2. High blood pressure, heart disease and diabetes, along with high blood sugar, cancer and diabetes are all factors.

3.Over-the-countercold/allergy medications,

4. Hormonal imbalance,

5. Trouble in the marriageanger towards your partner

6. Smoking/alcohol/illegal drugs,

7. You are single and without a partner

...and so on.

Take a look back at the last time that you had sex with someone in the basement. How did the rest? Did you notice the same thing happening in other areas? As if you were hitting a brick wall regardless of what you did?

There are three options for launching an out-of body experience.

If you interact with an energy in one of these ways, you're also exchanging energy. Your energy transfers to them and their energy transfers back to you. Connect only with people you trust. If you decide to connect with someone less than conscientious, you will make their energy part of your own until you do an energy cleansing.

Is OBE sex considered to be cheating?

This question is frequently asked by those in sexless or loveless relationships. It would be considered cheating if he or she does not keep up with the OBE sex relationship. Cheating can only be determined by the partner.

OBE sex is pure, unadulterated energy. There are no physical parts that merge. Every person sees cheating in a different way. For some it's sharing personal data, while for others it's a kiss and sexual intercourse. OBE sex may be a good option for sexless couples. The intense OBE encounters can turn your body on to such an extent that you will want to share your feelings with your partner. OBE sex doesn't replace sex. In a healthy relationship it is additive sex. OBE can help to reignite love feelings in a loving relationship.

OBE sex can be different from phone or online sex. People usually use online/phone sex to avoid having to have sex. Two people using different phones/computers are getting each other off to achieve real orgasm.

The person who was involved in the phone/computer sex did not want to have sexual relations with their partner. This is simply my point of view. Each individual must arrive at their conclusion.

White Light Protection

You don't need to have birth control while OBE sex is legal. That kind of protection is not what I mean. What you really need is protection from lower energies.

For OBE, you can surround yourself with bright white light to keep you safe. It's very easy. Simply close your eyes and picture the sky opening and surrounding you in bright, white light. Keep the image in your mind for a few moments, and then you'll be on your own.

Preparing your Inner Light

To prepare for or to increase your inner light, before you begin on the path of OBE experiences, it is a good idea. The inner fire, which is also our soul, is essential. It is vital that it be strengthened. Although it is bright and beautiful at birth, our souls are stuffed with crap throughout our lives. Stuff like "I can't be alone for the rest" or "I have no worth."

Each derogatory word can cloud our inner light. The self-imposed crap heap is making it more difficult to see the light.

You will attract lower energies to your OBE experiences if you have a dim light. This is how I talk about intimacy power. If you have sex (obe sex or real), your energies can mix. To attract higher vibrational souls/people, you need to keep your energy vibrating high.

Techniques for preparing your inner light

1. Be free from self-destructive beliefs and thoughts. You can summon angels, guides, and whatever other divine energy you need to remove your negative feelings. Loudly command your thoughts and beliefs to be taken away. I'm done with them! It helps me to think of a shovel removing my throat, heart and solar plexus chakras in order to release a lot of black goo into this Universe.

2. You can be conscious of your thoughts. Push any negative thoughts or self-limiting views out of your mind.

3. You should think about what makes your happy. Even more critical: FEEL the happiness associated to the thought.

4. White light does not just serve to protect you. Imagine the white glow emanating from your insides radiating outward. Your physical body, in the middle a white-light solar. This boosts your energy!

Preparing for your Energy

Preparing for OBE sex is an excellent idea. The following tips may help you connect with OBE sex more easily if you have trouble making a connection.

Take a soak in the tub or take a shower. It will help you to perform better and improve your concentration. Your energy and the energy around your body will feel cleaner when you feel it.

Drinking alcohol and using prescription drugs must be stopped at least six hours before OBE. It does not add to the experience. They do relax you. However, they also blur the lines between hallucinations/reality and make it difficult for you to remember the experience.

Don't feel hungry or thirsty. It can distract you from the task in hand.

Red meat must be avoided at all costs for twelve hours before OBE. Red meat grounds your energy. OBE is more difficult when you eat red meat.

A diet high in organic fruits and veggies is a good idea.

For increased focus, memory, brainpower, you might want to try at least one these herbs. However, it is a good idea to talk with your doctor before trying any of them.

Bacopa Meniere is a herb that boosts the mind, reduces anxiety and depression and improves cognitive and memory function.

Ginkgo Biloba, it improves blood flow to the legs. It also increases blood flow in the ears, brain and legs. This can help with memory. Ginkgo Biola can also help those who are taking medication for depression and anxiety.

GMO (Genetically Modified Organisms), should be avoided. GMO-altered foods can make this difficult as many commercial foods are made with GMO grains. GMOs can make it hard to get OBE and also make it harder for you to stay healthy. You can view a list of companies that you should avoid at your grocery store.

Comfortable clothing is recommended.

Do not start your day without at least 10 minutes of meditation or daydreaming. This helps to calm the mind and eliminate any clutter from your daily life that may interfere with your energy flow.

Chapter 17: Deadly Astral Projection between Science & Hypothesis

Is there another reality to our five senses than we perceive? Are we able to develop this knowledge and wisdom as individuals or as a species?

These deep questions are answered emphatically by Anne and Whitley Schtrieber, the inspiring authors of The Afterlife Revolution.

I have enjoyed many books on near-death experiences as well as after-death communications. I have contributed forewords to some of these books. I have also written a few books about spiritual science, including The Afterlife Experiments. Experiments.

In its overall scope, beauty, as well as lessons for all, the Afterlife Revolution stands apart from other books. Despite the many controversy surrounding these extraordinary authorssuch as their reported observations about aliensor perhaps because of their historic openness towards intelligent life beyond Earth, Anne's story takes on an additional significance and meaning after Anne's death.

To honor the inspiring nature and breadth of Anne and Whitleys relationship, both before and following Anne's passing, and their shared intellectual curiosity about life and the cosmos, I felt compelled by this book to write a preface. This foreword will address the importance love and especially real love.

I was forced to write this preface because of the unexpected and compelling evidence that Anne was present in my personal and professional lives.

Let's begin by looking at this amazing evidence of Anne's presence, and then move on to the Afterlife Revolution. I have given enough information to allow you to understand and assess the persuasive nature of the evidence.

Rhonda (my wife), and I were getting ready to drive to Scottsdale (Arizona) on Thursday morning, September 14th 2017. There I would be giving two presentations for the Afterlife Research and Education Institute Conference. (www. afterlifestudies.org). Friday's lecture was titled "Lessons learned from mediumship science in spirit communication technology research." Saturday's banquet presentation was titled "How science shows that spirits collaborate with us."

Coast AM host George Nory co-hosted the evening banquet. Whitley co-authored a bestselling work with Art Bell (previous award-winning host Coast-to-Coast AM). Their book, The Coming Global Superstorm, was the inspiration for The Day After Tomorrow.

When I started The Afterlife Revolution, I had the idea that perhaps I could get independent evidence about Anne's continued consciousness.

Science generally affirms there is no soul. However, neuroscience confirms that there is no evidence of an afterlife. Bereavement Hallucinations is the term for contact with the dead. The scientific community believes that the only truth that matters is the reality that can be detected with existing instruments.

Oliver Sacks talks about afterlife communications in his book

Hallucinations. He doesn't think they are hallucinations.

Science is a marvel of the human mind. Over the past three hundred years, it has applied theory and discovered new phenomena to provide ever more valuable insights. However, if there are no data, the system is unable to recognize them.

Voltaire, the 18th-century scientist, dismissed fossils as fish bones left behind by travelers. For years scientists had denied the existence of meteors, saying that stones cannot fall from the skies. However, fossils too large for fish bones were eventually found and meteors were tracked to their ground.

As Voltaire did not have sufficient data to justify his investigation of fossils, scientists do not have enough data about the soul. Science also does no possess any instrument capable of convincingly detecting it. Scientists are now assuming that it does not exist. It is not the soul that doesn't die, but an instrument which can detect it.

Two impediments stand in the way for such a device's development. Science is a well-respected field. It is a towering institution that declares the soul not exists. This leads to us, even those who believe otherwise, questioning our own soul experiences and sometimes filtering them out.

The fundamental human question is "Will it be possible to live on after death?" This is a simple, universal question that haunts everyone. Science's insistence that we are mortal flesh reinforces our fear about annihilation. Simultaneously with the increasing complexity and vibrancy of our material world, it makes it more difficult to hear the subtle inner voice within us.

However, even though many are giving up on their souls, there are many voices proclaiming that there is a afterlife. Pimm Van Lomeli wrote an article in the Annals of the New York Academy of Sciences stating that 9 million people had experienced near-death experiences. Anne was one example of such a person. She, like so many others, returned to this life without fear of death. She was brought back by medical technology, like many.

It is paradoxical that the science that says that the soul does not exist is also responsible one of many foundations of this afterlife revolution.

Anne will share her new life through our narrative in ways I find revelatory. She was articulate and brought all her expressive skills to her portrayal of life on her side. You shouldn't expect to hear stories about warm light. It's a complicated world with nuance and ambiguity that she describes, which is why it's also quite shocking.

This species will find a new, more reliable method of contact and, in doing so, will awaken to its true purpose of existence. Although there is much joy in the afterlife revolution it will require a gentle approach. Anne said, "The hardest thing to do in the afterlife revolution is to let it be fun." The good news is that once you do it, it will be easy.

Hypothesis

This is the afterlife Revolution, a journey to a new evolution in humanity and a totally new living experience.

But how do you go about it? How do we get back in touch with our souls and those who are already gone? They are where? What do they want? What do they want and need?

Anne has carried out a plan that was laid years ago. This has proven that Anne still exists. She did it in support of the great mission, which she is now a member of, to bring this species together in a totally new way. What is it that she has done to be able this feat? Is there a special thing about her that makes it possible? Or is it that she is simply using a skill that is part and parcel of every human being, and showing me how to use it as well?

We will explore these topics together and demonstrate how the skill that we are using can be applied in all aspects of our lives and relationships. We can create a bridge between our worlds and be more competent, peaceful, happier species.

Anne and my vote for this future are united by our shared vision of the bridge connecting the worlds. Of course, there will be challenges as a result of all the changes that are taking place on Earth. We have seen glimpses of the possibilities, and they seem more wonderful than our most optimistic theories.

Now, we face pressure from situations that are similar to those of our distant ancestors. They went through tough times to achieve a new life. One hundred thousand years ago, naked wanderers, the world was entering the last ice ages. They learned to cover themselves and language. They also had the ability to form tribes that were experts in all things they needed for survival.

We are going again to find our path into a new existence. This time, however, it will be truly different. As we learn to live in and beyond the material world, we move into an expansive reality which is just beginning to open up to us. The new humanity, complete, is finally possible.

This book is about that journey.

The fundamental reality of the afterlife revolution lies in the fact that she lived to tell her story. Medical science had saved her and allowed her to recount her near-death story rather than disappearing into an unknown.

They were considered to be rare and remarkable because they had entered the worlds of the dead and were resurrected. These stories are still the core of many religious beliefs and practices. The Tibetan Book of the Dead, and the Egyptian Pyramid Texts, are based upon observations made during such journeys. However, they are not suitable texts for our times. Although the stories of the adventures they tell are told in terms that were familiar to the time, the mythology they use is not applicable to modern times.

Chapter 18: The Scientific Hypothesis

Is life after death real? Is there more to reality than our five senses can perceive? Are we able to develop this knowledge and wisdom as individuals, and as a species? The energy of chanting and rhythmic breathing can help you to see, hear and feel the astral world. It emits a ringing sound at different pitches. You may hear a click or snap, which can feel almost like electricity coursing through your body. You can feel it in the screen between your eyes. It seems like your eyes contain an energy.

If this happens, get mental" and move both your fingers as well as your toes. You don't have to go to these extreme emotional states. It's easy to project your emotions outwardly and inwardly. Once you become used to this feeling, you will realize that it is not a negative sign. It simply means that you have an abundance energy.

Astral projection and meditation increase the likelihood that you will spontaneously experience signs of an alternate reality in your daily life. Although you might hear voices and experience a ringing or flashing light, these are not indications that your mind, ears, or eyes have problems. Accept this new reality and accept it as a blessing. But, keep in control. If the distractions become overwhelming or excessive, be loud and insist that they go.

For a while, it took me several sessions to gain the required momentum. Group sessions are more energetic because we all have astral energy and can share it immediately. These group sessions can be stressful if not all members are familiar with each other and if a trusted member is there to oversee the gathering. Even though it sounds unbelievable, we sometimes project more than one at a time. Although it sounds absurd, it is quite true.

If you are in deep trance, for example, you may see yourself flying. Because you are not centered within that energy, it is possible to be discouraged. This was a frequent occurrence for me.

There was a part of me that kept my eyes closed to allow me to breathe. The projection flew into the sky. But there was also a part that observed. It took me a while before I realized that I had projected two bodies astral and that my eyes were centered on the observer. To enjoy my astral projection adventures, I had to change the direction of my gaze and my focus. It was much easier to make my travels vivid and more exciting after I did that.

It is also common to have several astral projections. But, instead of being centered in the outgoing energies at all, this power stays behind and breathes lightly so you don't retain any memories. A projection will leave your physical body and you will notice if it is gone. You will then feel tired and chilled. The projection will eventually return and you will feel rejuvenated. Sometimes it even starts. This could happen because of a projection that originated from the dream state.

Air Quality

You should also consider the quality and quantity of the air you are breathing. It is best to have enough healthy oxygen.

It is now common knowledge that in order to preserve heat inside a house, you must seal all windows, doors, attic, and roofs so heat doesn't escape. This leads to us breathing the same old air over and over again. You should open your windows throughout the day to allow fresh air to circulate around your home. It is obvious that meditation will improve your health and will make you feel more relaxed.

The exchange of atoms within the air we breathe makes us all very connected on this earth. These atoms hold our essence and all of the others, so they touch on the astral level and higher. By practicing spiritual meditation, you can increase the vibrations and blessings of the atoms you breathe. It's up to us to decide if the wind spreads light and happiness, or gloom.

Sometimes, subconscious minds project a factor that we have captured into our sleep. Imagine that you have an ingrained habit of going to a certain place. The subconscious will not forget it. If the subconscious mind gets the idea from the subconscious, it will trigger you to take action if this impression is strong enough.

It will happen if there are other factors like temperament or weakness of your physical body that favor this projection. While it is believed there is an astral projection, it may also be due to a specific reason. The reason she was called sudden is unknown. Even though they cause projection at the appropriate temperament, an average habit and a common desire don't leave enough imprints in the subconscious mind. An old habit and an intense desire are better imprinted and are therefore more effective. In reality, they are deeply rooted in your subconscious mind. The same applies to abandoned habits and suppressed wishes. When a habit becomes deeply rooted in the subconscious mind it is then that the mind learns how to express it. He seems to be trying desperately to express it. This is why they are so difficult to let go of. If you have a particular habit, and you want to get rid of it, your subconscious mind will start to show it more than usual. The tension within you is felt, so the subconscious will attempt to move the astral bodies to carry out the desired action. It works in the same way that suppressed desires work. You must be able to satisfy that desire. If you are unable to satisfy it, then you should make conscious effort to stop yourself from pursuing your inner desires. If there was an obstacle, you would instantly quench your desire. The subconscious must be charged in order for the astral bodies to move. If this happens, then how will it be able to control the body? Scientists estimate that the average astral body weighs around two ounces. Imagine a person with a 160-pound body. This is the body's physical weight. It is 1280x heavier than the astral. However, it can be started by one simple suggestion. The subconscious will follow the same suggestion to set the body of the astral during sleep, even if it is in a dream. If subconscious willpower is used to follow established orders, the order becomes permanent in the subconscious mind. But a dream follows a suggestion and not like a subject who has been hypnotized.